LAND REFORM
MYTHS AND REALITIES

About the Author

Dr. Amit Hazra (b. 1963) is a Reader in Economics in the Department of Social Studies and Rural Development, Visva-Bharati University. He did his Post-Graduation from the State Agricultural University (Bidhan Chandra Krishi Viswavidyalaya) and has received his Ph.D. from Visva-Bharati. He joined the Department in 1993 and has attended a number of national and international seminars, conferences and symposiums. Dr. Hazra has published more than 20 articles in international and national journals of repute. He has also acted as the Vice-Principal of the Institute of Rural Reconstruction, Visva-Bharati. His areas of specialization are rural development methodologies like PRA/PLA, participatory development and sustainable rural development.

LAND REFORMS
MYTHS AND REALITIES

Amit Hazra

CONCEPT PUBLISHING COMPANY, NEW DELHI-110059

Cataloging in Publication Data—DK
Courtesy: D.K. Agencies (P) Ltd. <docinfo@dkagencies.com>

Hazra, Amit, 1963-
Land reforms : myths and realities / Amit Hazra.
p. cm.
Study conducted at Birbhum, Burdwan and Jalpaiguri districts of West Bengal, India.
Includes bibliographical references (p.)
Includes index.
ISBN 8180693074

1. Land reform—India—West Bengal. I. Title.

DDC 333.315 4 22

ISBN 81-8069-307-4

First Published 2006

Published and Printed by
Ashok Kumar Mittal
Concept Publishing Company
A/15-16, Commercial Block, Mohan Garden
New Delhi-110059 (INDIA)

Phones : 25351460, 25351794
Fax : 091-11-25357103
Email : publishing@conceptpub.com

Preface

A sound land reform policy can contribute significantly to agriculture and rural development, and therefore deserves high priority. The land policy should be such that it ensures the scientific and intensive use of land, creates productive employment, reduces disparities in the distribution of land, provides incentives to increase productivity of land, and induces changes in property relations and social structure, with a view to enabling the wider participation of landowners and tenants in the process of sustainable rural development.

After Independence, the Government of India formulated a comprehensive land reforms policy for the first time in the First Five Year Plan. The main objectives of the policy were to remove such impediments to the modernization of agriculture as were innate in the agrarian structure inherited from the past, and reduction of gross inequalities in the agrarian economy. It accorded a high priority to programmes that increased agricultural production, promoted diversification, reduced disparities in income and wealth, eliminated exploitation, and provided security to tenants. Necessary land reform legislation has already been enacted by the respective state governments, and is now in force. The policy and the programmes have been periodically reviewed and evaluated. Many glaring gaps have occurred between the objectives of the policy and the legislation enacted to achieve them, and between the laws and their enforcement.

In this comprehensive book 'Land Reforms : Myths and Realities' an attempt has been made to explore the actual scenario of West Bengal's much-discussed and debated "Operation Barga" on a broad canvas. For the purpose, I have set out a broad historical overview of landholding and cropping relations in both pre- as well as post-Independence India. Tracing the roots of this internationally acclaimed land reform movement to Gandhiji's pronouncements in pre-Independence India and relating it to larger socio-historical and theoretical issues, this study tried to discuss the expectations and achievements of land reforms in revitalizing the present agrarian system in the era of decolonisation.

This work begins from basic definitions of land and agrarian reform, goes on to discuss the debates about their possible (and actual) efficacy, follows up with a discussion of the pros and cons of land reform, and surveys a wealth of information on the constitutional and legal framework of such reforms, before narrowing its focus to the actual practice and effects of land reform in the context of West Bengal's 'Operation Barga' in three districts—Birbhum, Bardhaman and Jalpaiguri—with distinct ecological, agricultural, social and economic histories and contexts of the state.

A detailed chronology of review work on Land Reforms especially on Barga system in West Bengal has been provided to enumerate the failures as well as the successes of the land reform process in the state.

By far the most comprehensive and interesting part of the work are the detailed case studies and analyses of the deviations from the system of Operation Barga and for what reasons. This not only helps the reader to gauge how Operation Barga has affected (and may affect) the political economy of a village, but also to understand the complex effects of this land reform movement on sharecroppers, and small, marginal and large farmers.

Although sympathetic to the idea of land reform and the role it can play in the development of a nation and the uplift of its people, I remained careful to point out how the actual operation of a land reform movement has sometimes gone against the interests of those it was expressly designed to serve. But this exploration, by no way, leads to question the process or, indeed, the desirability of land reform. Quite the contrary, I really want the state to develop mechanisms to make the system of land reform "foolproof". This study identifies the areas that need further intervention and policies that need to be reviewed and, if necessary, revamped, particularly in view of the changes that have taken place in the global economy as a whole.

March 10, 2005 **Amit Hazra**

Acknowledgements

While conducting the study I received valuable co-operation, guidance and encouragement from different quarters, which I would like to acknowledge at the outset.

The book is based on a project work on Land Reforms sponsored by the University Grants Commission. I am really grateful to the UGC for giving me opportunity to carry out such a project, which needs crucial intervention by the policy makers and thinkers on land reforms in India. In this connection I acknowledge the works of eminent scholars, academicians and organisations in this field which gave me immense opportunity to compile their ideas and views in the book.

I would like to place on record my heartfelt gratitude to the facilitators of my study at the district, block, Gram Panchayat and village levels. To mention only a few, the Offices of the District Land and Land Reform Officers of Birbhum, Burdwan and Jalpaiguri; Offices of the Block Development Officers of Dubrajpur, Memari-II and Falakata; Offices of the Gram Panchayats of Jashpur, Kuchut and Dhanirampur and, in particular, the villagers of the twelve study villages in the respective Gram Panchayats.

I am thankful to my friend Dr. Samantak Das, Reader in English, Jadavpur University, for careful reading of the content of the book and his candid suggestions to improve the literature of the book.

I am also thankful to my students who constituted the research team—Dr. Sujay Mitra, Sri Subhrangsu Santra, Sri Rajesh Chatterjee and Sri Dibyendu Ghosh.

I am thankful to Prof. Somnath Chakravorty, Dr. Bijay Mukherjee, Sri Amlan Datta Mandal and Sri Susanta Chakravorty for their valuable suggestions to develop the material of this book.

Last but not the least, my sincere gratitude and acknowledgements go to my respected parents, my wife Smt. Mithu Hazra and my son Sriman Anindya for their cooperation and constant encouragement to complete this hard task. They have been the primary inspiration behind my work.

Sriniketan **Amit Hazra**
February 10, 2004

Contents

List of Tables

1

Land Reforms: A Retrospect

Land reform is a debatable issue. The debate has been inspired by passionate polemics as well as by scientific inquiry. Thus, some argue that land reform is needed to preserve democracy and political stability, while others consider it as a threat to democracy and free enterprise. Again, from 'reformism' point of view, some say that it is the best way of preserving essential economic and institutional features, while others, from Marxist (revolutionary) point of view, argue that it is needed to bring structural (capitalist) transformation of the society, by smashing the exploitative rural power structure.

The divergence, nevertheless, arises largely from varying political and ideological points of view. Taking cognizance to all varieties of view points, our main concern here is to develop an integrated approach to analyse the whole process of agrarian change *vis-à-vis* the essential ingredient of the pattern of reform over a wide span of time.

It is by now widely acknowledged that political power structure in poor agrarian economies is largely based on the land ownership/operational pattern of the rural households. This land ownership/operational pattern releases a set of forces that determines the relationship between various classes of farmers. This relationship is better termed as land relation which in turn is linked to political power relationship. If this relationship (say, landlord-tenant) acts as an impediment to the development of productive forces, reform is needed to change this relationship for transforming the structure of the agrarian economies of impoverished developing countries. This indicates that the process of agrarian reform is inherently a political process.

The underlying importance of land reform is to change the exploitative land relations for the development of productive forces. Thus land reform in a nutshell constitutes a strategy of development, which is based on an institutional framework where due to change in land (production) relations, the cultivator can get the fruits of labour. This occurs in such a fashion that cultivators now feel tempted or get incentive to increase their surplus so as to use it for productive purposes as efficiently as possible in speeding up the growth of the economy as a whole (Mohalanobis, 1963). That is to say, we have to develop a "growth strategy" as opposed to "growth-oriented strategy" as a promoter of economic growth built in within the programme of land reform. In this context, land reform is treated as the engine of surplus generation through which continuous growth of productive forces takes place (Mohalanobis, 1963).

The above arguments thus suggest that agricultural/rural development may broadly be based on two approaches. One is technological and the other is institutional or structural. Land reform, no doubt, constitutes the institutional or structural approach. It is to be noted here that change in land relations consequent upon the adoption of land reform measures does not bring automatic development of productive forces. For that development, relentless efforts of adopting technological and institutional factors are to be emphasized for transformation of the society at a higher plane.

For the development of the economy as a whole, we cannot isolate one sector (say, agriculture) from another sector (say, industry). The industrial bourgeoisie cannot remain apathetic to the programme of land reform so long as this programme can remove the wage goods (supplied by agriculture) constraints and crisis of effective demand for industrial goods and associated services. However, the solution of the crisis can, nevertheless, be reached by an expansion of domestic market backed by an increase of rural purchasing power as an effect of land reform measures. But the industrial bourgeoisie would prefer the strategy without reform (e.g. Green Revolution strategy), if his problems were solved by that strategy. Because his preferred strategy would allow him to avoid the possible conflicts with the landlord and rural rich. Indian experience of green revolution strategy shows that such a preference revealed by the industrial bourgeoisie could not be arrived at due to the failure of the green revolution strategy for bringing about sufficient production, income and employment in the agrarian sector (Chakravorty, 1979). This indicates that even the industrial bourgeoisie who would have usual support to their allies (e.g., landlord, rich farmer) in rural sector cannot avoid the inevitability of land reform.

The primary motivation of land reform is to reduce poverty by reducing inequality. This, however, cannot be achieved by no less than distributive measures. The redistributive land reform is advocated, because smaller farms exhibit higher employment and output. Thus redistributed land reform measures are often justified on the ground of efficiency, equity and justice. On the ground of non-feasibility and non-availability of sufficient land to distribute and non-viability of holding, redistributive land reform is often considered to be 'utopian'. For these reasons, some argue for structural reorganization, but come up with tenurial reform. Tenancy reforms are, however, argued on the ground that share tenancy is inefficient in both static (production) and dynamic (saving/surplus utilization/investment) senses. As a matter of fact, suggested tenancy reform in isolation cannot go for any desired change, so long as the high incidence of tenancy and the exploitative nature of land market emanate from highly unequal land ownership structure.

The above arguments suggest that radically redistributive land reform is not utopian. Ironically, misconception is cropped up when the twin concerns of redistributive land reform and tenancy reform are treated to be anti-empirical and anti-historical radicalism (Rahman, 1994). This so-called realistic approach of land administration as the priority agenda of land reform can hardly go beyond the bureaucratization of efforts to form a struggle against the powerfully entrenched vested interest. The approach of smashing absentee landlords without resorting to redistributive measures as suggested by Umar (1982) for the development of capitalism in agriculture appears to be erroneous. Because highly unequal landownership pattern will invite absentee owners to sustain so much so that feudalistic remnants will inhibit the prospect of capitalist development in agriculture.

The concepts of non-feasibility, non-viability and non-availability of land in the context of distributive land reform measures appear as static and mechanical. We are quite aware that in a land scarce economy, enough land will not be available. What is more important is not the amount of land, but number of peasants who would be the owners of land and would unleash their creative energy to put an end to the stranglehold of the anti-productive vested interest. This is a process, which helps complete the task of bourgeoisie democratic revolution (Konar, 1980, Khasnabis, 1986). And for this reason, we have to rely much on the support of the peasantry and civil society.

Furthermore, empirical evidence by now suggest that drastic land reform followed by cooperatisation and collectivization as a long run measures, may facilitate economies of scale, the large-scale introduction of modern technology, increased production and larger agricultural surplus (Siddique, 1979). For the short run, in absence of such cooperatisation and/or collectivization, any land redistribution programme may even promote small holding agriculture successfully by providing credit and modern inputs effectively (Bose, 1974 and Joshi, 1987).

Moreover, the question of land reform has to be looked from the whole spectrum of market and production relations. For that matter, the notion of surplus is an appropriate concept in the context of developing agrarian societies. Thus, in the plane of production relations, two sets of mutually contradictory strategies (e.g. 'survival strategy' on the part of impoverished peasants and labourers and 'surplus appropriation strategy' involving direct intervention in production process by the part of landlords-traders-money lenders) may be in operation to provide the basis for identifying the general characteristics of an agrarian system. Bringing fundamental changes in certain indicators) e.g. growth, income distribution, employment generation etc.) may, therefore, involve a transition from one economic system to another. Land reform thus needs to be viewed as an instrument for affecting such transition (Ghose 1983).

Land although a gift of nature like air and sunshine, has shown a tendency since time immemorial, to pass under the control of individuals as their personal asset. This process helped the growth of a system of exploitation broadly known as feudalism. Most modern developed countries embarked on their path of industrialization and economic development only after completing some form of land reform and agrarian reform.

After the Second World War, as imperialism collapsed, a large number of countries in Asia and Africa became independent and many governments of the newly independent countries initiated economic development programmes. A common ingredient to these programmes was emphasise on the need for speedy land reform. India and other countries of the subcontinent were not different from this pattern.

Land reform basically means breaking up of large land holdings and redistribution of land to landless and small owners. This is also an essential precondition for increasing productivity of land and labour in agriculture. In the Indian context, land reform initially meant abolition of Zamindari and reform of tenurial system. Although the Indian National Congress brought the problem of Zamindari abolition to the forefront as early as 1928, the *modus operandi* of such a step was not spelt out. Gandhi was however very straightforward on this issue. In 1937 he wrote, "All land belongs to Gopal". He also indicated how the people could recover their ownership of land – "I have no doubt we can make as good an approach as is possible for any nation, not excluding Russia, and that without violence ..... Land and all property is his who will work on it."

On the eve of the 'Quit India' movement Gandhi expressed his idea in course of a discussion with Louis Fischer about agrarian reforms in free India. "The peasant world take the land. We would not have to tell them to take it". On the question of compensation to the landlords he said, "that would be fiscally impossible". His views represented the dominant aspiration of the rural poor masses awakened by the rising anti-imperialist sentiment but as the time of transfer of power or independence appeared closer the Congress leaders started talking about land reform in a 'realistic' manner. Thus the Congress election-manifesto of 1946 stated, "The reform of the land system which is so urgently needed in India, involves the removal of intermediates between the peasants and the State. The rights of such intermediaries would therefore, be acquired on pavement of equitable compensation."

The report of the Congress Agrarian Reforms Committee (1949), which guided all subsequent land reform acts passed by the Congress ministries in different states made a peculiar compromise on the question of 'Rights on land'. "The committee suggested sharing of the rights on land between the community and the tiller. The idea of proprietorship was declared incongruous and the state taking overall authority was rejected as injurious to the development of individual initiative and personalities". The committee suggested permanent, transferable and heritable right of cultivation to the cultivator subject to certain conditions, which did not include actual tilling of land.

It is well recognized that in the battle against hunger and poverty, land reform is an effective weapon. In a country where about seventy percent of the population is dependent on agriculture for their livelihood, and in a rural economy dominated by small and marginal farmers and poor agricultural workers, land is a precious asset, which has to be put to optimum use to get maximum benefit for the target number.

Land Reforms: An Initiation

Fifty-two years after the first ideals of poverty and inequality mitigation were set before the country, nearly a billion—39 per cent live below the poverty line—without the basic amenities of living. While total foodgrain productivity increased nearly fourfold from 1950-51 to 1996-97, it is still considered to be performing below its true potential and will certainly fall inadequate for the burgeoning rate at which population is growing. As in 1990-91, the bottom 59.99 per cent marginal farmers operated only 14.87 per cent of the total cropped area, while the top 1.59 per cent of large farmers operated as much as 17.45 per cent land.

In a predominantly rural country like India, where nearly three-fourth of the nation live in rural areas, most of those below the poverty line are also rural based. The poorest sections of Indian society belong to the landless and marginal rural-agricultural categories. Poverty as a situation has remained by and large static over the decades of industrial development and green revolution, despite of the fact that it receives the widest political patronage and developmental coverage in the country. An inadequate land reform feeds poverty in two ways—by lowering both productivity and motivational inputs for increasing productivity.

Of the total working population 64.8 per cent are dependent on agriculture. This 64.8 per cent, however, contributes to only 27.4 per cent of the GDP. Various reasons can be cited for the relatively low productivity of Indian farmers. These include inadequate irrigation facilities, inefficient cropping pattern, lack of distribution mechanisms for seeds and fertilizers, lack of mechanization and natural calamities. Another, very important set of reasons for low yield are the outdated agrarian practices. Such practices like large landholdings, unregulated tenancy, fragmented holdings etc. lower output, which in turn is linked to poverty.

Besides the productivity argument, another perhaps more important facet of the land question is that of equity. Continued emphasis was given on the socialist ideals of the country in the Five-Year Plans and political agendas of the governments in power. The average size of holdings for marginal farmers – those owing lands below 1 hectare is 0.40 hectares, while the large landholders own an average of 17.30 hectares. The economic, social and politico-cultural disabilities that characterize any society with marked disparities in landholdings are well known. They include, among others, inequalities in access to health, education and the rural power structure. The reasons for our country's low ranking in terms of the human development can also be traced to the disparity in landholding pattern.

The bedrock of facts, upon which three related issues—poverty, relatively low agricultural output, and inequity are based, can thus be seen to revolve around the pivot called land rights and use.

The significance of the concept of land reforms in achieving our goals of social life was recognized much before, but national level programmes, policies, and legislation for land reform was given shape only after 1947. Thought the implementation of such efforts left much to be wanted, land reform as an issue seems to have lost the kind of attention it deserves. In such a situation, it is first necessary to see why land reform is the most vital need to address these problems.

All efforts at reform in land ownership have as their goal the more equitable redistribution of land. Land reform measures like land ceiling diffuses the uneconomic consequences of unequal (very small versus very large) landholdings. Levels of health, nutrition, education, access to irrigation and basic sanitation all show a positive relationship with land ownership sizes.

Whenever rentals take up a major part of income from land, and land is held as a closed investment, tenants have very little incentive or opportunity to increase the productive capacity of land. Thus bringing the State into direct contact with the tillers not only increases their self-worth, but also goes a long way into bettering the quality of land and crop growing practices, leading to increased productivity.

The small/marginal landowners, tenants and the landless quite often have unequal access to the use of common natural resources in the rural areas. In addition, their involvement in the local decision making processes gets relegated to the background. They are also sometimes deprived from institutional facilities and developmental activities introduced by the government for the rural poor due to various reasons including non-awareness.

Redistribution of land is thus widely looked upon both a goal as well as means to achieve greater equity, self-respect and self-confidence towards meeting livelihood needs for the families of the categories of the rural poor, at the same time serving the wider interests of increased food security and agricultural productivity for the nation as a whole.

Concepts of Land Reforms

Three terms frequently used in any discussion on land reforms. They are – land reform, agrarian reform, and land right. It is necessary to take a closer look at these key concepts.

Land Reform is a term used to mean a wide variety of specific measures and programmes. It has been broadly defined by the Encyclopaedia Britannica as "a specific integrated-action programme to bring about more effective control and use of land for the direct benefit of the community as a whole". In a narrower sense, land reform comprises of (i) the compulsory take over of land, usually by the State from the biggest land owners with partial compensation, and (ii) the farming of that land in such a way as to spread the benefits of the man-land relationship more widely than before take over.

Land reforms can be interpreted as the means to bring about a change in the agrarian structure towards equity and increased productivity. This structure includes the man-land relationship (control over land), man-man relationship on land (i.e. between tenants and landlords) and land development as such. The Indian ideal of land reform is socialistic as well as democratic. The reforms are envisaged to be achieved through the following five measures: abolition of intermediaries, tenancy reforms, ceiling on landholdings, consolidation and encouraging cooperatives.

Agrarian reform is a term often used interchangeable with land reform. It is a broader term, embracing the entire agrarian structure, besides covering the elements of land reform, including measures for the modernization of agricultural practices and the improvement of the living conditions of the entire agrarian population. Thus agrarian reform covers the establishment of cooperatives and other institutions for supplying agricultural credit and other inputs; processing and marketing of agricultural produce; establishment of agro-industries; agricultural workers.

Land right is another related concept, defined as legally and socially recognized claims on land enforceable by an external legitimized authority. Rights in land can be in the form of ownership or usufruct, associated with different degrees of freedom to lease out, mortgage, bequeath, or sell. Land rights can stem from inheritance of an individual or joint family, from community membership, transfers by the state, or from tenancy arrangements, purchase, and so on.

Constitutional Position of Land Reforms

Land reform is a State subject in the Constitution of India. It falls under Entry 18 of the State List which covers: "Lands, that is to say, rights in or over land, land tenures including the relations of landlord and tenant, and the collection of rents, transfer and alienation of agricultural lands, land improvement and agricultural loans. In effect, it implies that only the state governments can enact laws over these matters related to land.

Part IV of the Directive Principles of State Policy also refers to the objectives contained in the programme for land reforms, though it directs so indirectly. This is evident from the following clauses:

- Clause (a)—the citizens, men and women equally, have the right to an adequate means of livelihood;
- Clause (b)—the ownership and control of the resources of the community are so distributed as to subserve the common good;
- Clause (c)—the operation of the economic systems does not result in the concentration of wealth and means of production to the common detriment.

The tenuous constitutional basis for the Central Government's role in land reforms is Entry 20 in the Concurrent List, which speaks of Social and Economic Planning. This entry is the sole constitutional basis for establishment of the Planning Commission, whose role in land reform has necessarily been of an advisory nature. It can only lay down the general principles or guidelines for legislation and implementation in the Five-Year Plans.

Objectives of Land Reforms

The **Primary objectives** of the land reforms programme are to do away with the inequities prevalent in the system of landholding and to increase productivity. The First Five Year Plan enunciated the purpose of the policies as, firstly, to remove such motivational and other impediments to increase in agricultural production as arise from the agrarian structure inherited from the past, and, secondly, to eliminate of exploitation and social injustice within the agrarian system so as to ensure equality of status and opportunity to all sections of the rural population.

The **secondary objectives** are linked to the specific measures. Intermediaries were sought to be abolished so as to end the exploitative practices that the real tillers of the soil were subjected to; as well as to enable the redistribution of lands from the hands of parasitic middlemen to the tillers themselves. Ceiling on agricultural holdings endeavoured to ensure that ownership of land does not get concentrated in a few hands. A tenancy reform seeks to give rights to tenants or, as in the case of Assam and Bihar abolishes tenancy altogether so that all farmers till their own land. Landholdings are consolidated with the goal of increasing productivity by making mechanization possible. Over successive Plans, these objectives were revised and supplemented with many others.

Efforts in Land Reforms

Altering the man-land relations and the man-man relations on land has been a concern for centuries both with decision-makers and commoners of a country or region. Ranging from direct, landlord-to-labourer confrontations, to remotely envisioned laws—attempts to control rights over land have taken myriad forms. Wherever the government policies have failed to protect rights of the non-owners, peasant and people's movements have targeted oppressors and policy makers to press for change. All such attempts of land reforms can be broadly categorized under four heads.

1. A top-down approach, which can be grouped as **government efforts**. This is mainly based on legislative support according to the policies of the central government. State governments enact the actual laws.
2. A bottom-upwards approach initiated by the people who are disadvantaged in the existing land relations, which can be termed as **peasant efforts**. These movements have often turned militant.
3. Action from below introduced by an individual, charismatic leaders or non-governmental organizations. Such **voluntary efforts** have always been an important way of initiating non-violent, consensus-based means to bringing about land reform.
4. Base on efforts of two or more of the three categories above, there have been **combined efforts**, as for instance a legislative provision that endorses peasant mobilization.

This general grouping of the Indian experiments in bringing about land reforms can now be dealt with at length to understand the scene more fully.

Governmental Action

Governmental efforts in land reform basically centres around the following five measures:

1. Abolition of intermediaries;
2. Tenancy reforms;
3. Ceiling on land holdings;
4. Consolidation of land holdings;
5. Legislations and their Implementation.

1. Abolition of Intermediaries

Laws to abolish intermediaries were passed almost simultaneously following Independence in 1947. By the end of the First Five-Year

Plan, all States had enacted laws for the abolition of intermediaries. The salient features of these laws were as follows:

- All laws brought the principal tenants on lands outside the intermediaries' home-farm into a direct relationship with the State. No limit was put on the area of the home-farm except in West Bengal, Assam, Hyderabad, Ajmer and Jammu and Kashmir.
- All laws provided for compensation to be paid to the ex-intermediaries. The rates of such compensation varied from 15 to 30 times the net annual income (for the lowest slab) to 12.5 to twice the net annual income (for the highest slab).

Implementation of the laws was delayed due to various reasons. Deliberate tactics were employed by the abolished intermediaries and the implementing agencies to hold up implementation. In several states, for instance, the ex-landlords challenged the laws in High Courts. The inherent delays in the judicial process were misused to the fullest extent, the most notorious of such cases being in the state of Bihar. The absence of reliable land records and the complexities of laws added to the woes of the potential beneficiaries.

Results of the laws to abolish intermediaries varied from state to state, but a few general comments can be made. The former intermediaries may continue as ordinary landlords on a fairly large scale, but their reign as semi-feudal chiefs in rural districts has come to an end. Despite the opposition and administrative and technical problems, the Zamindari tenures were virtually abolished. About 25 million erstwhile tenants became landowners directly under the state. Large tracts of privately owned forestland and cultivable wasteland were also vested in the state.

On the flip side, the laws led to the large-scale eviction of tenants-at-will, under-tenants, and sharecroppers under the guise of resumption of land for self-cultivation. In some states like Rajasthan even superior tenants were ejected.

2. *Tenancy Reforms*

Different economics have defined share tenancy differently. Definitions by themselves reflect the differing viewpoints of economists on the issue of share tenancy. To begin with Adam Smith in his *Wealth of Nations* defines Metayers (share tenants) who, he suggests, succeeded the slave cultivators of ancient times.

"The proprietor furnished them with the seed, cattle, and instruments of husbandry, the whole stock, in short, necessary for cultivating the farm. The produce was divided equally between the proprietor and the farmer, after setting aside what was judged necessary for keeping up the stock, which was restored to the proprietor when the farmer either quitted, or was turned out of the farm" (Smith, 1969).

Thus, share tenancy is viewed as a contract between a landowner and a tenant where the tenant cultivates the landowner's land with his labour and all instruments of production are provided by the landowner.

Similarly Marshall in his *Principles of Economics* distinguishes the English system of fixed rental and the system of Metayer, which was prevalent in the great part of Latin Europe. According to Marshall, in the case of Metayer or holding land on shares "the land is divided into holdings, which the tenant cultivates by the labour of himself and his family, and sometimes though rarely, that of a few hired labourers, and for which the landlord supplies buildings, cattle, and sometimes even, farm implements" (Marshall, 1961).

Thus share tenancy is, according to Marshall, a resource adjustment mechanism between the labour of the tenant and the land and other implements of the landlord. It is to be noted that in the Smithian and Marshallian notions of share tenant, the tenant is a poor and impoverished tenant who lacks sufficient means of production to undertake self-cultivation and here the share of the tenant resembles wages paid in kind.

But Cheung, a noted proponent of the neo-classical approach belonging to the new school, those who embrace the so-called private rights doctrine, has given a more comprehensive definition. Cheung defines share tenancy as,

"Share tenancy is a land lease under which the rent paid by the tenant is a contracted percentage of the output yield per period of time. As a rule, the landowner provides land and the tenant provides labour; either party may provide other inputs. Share tenancy is thus share contracting, defined here as two or more individual parties combining privately owned resources for the production of certain mutually agreed outputs, the actual outputs to be shared according to certain mutually accepted percentages as returns to the contracting parties for their productive resources forsaken" (Cheung, 1969).

Thus, share tenancy is here viewed as a method of resource adjustment between two parties who have unequal resource endowments, and thereby makes production feasible. The terms and conditions of share tenancy are agreed upon on mutual consent and both the landowner and the tenant are narrated as equal partners in the share contract. Here the conflict between the interests of the landowner and the tenant is assumed away. The dominance of the landowner class over the tenants, i.e., the economic power relations necessary for the enforcement of contract is ignored.

There is another variant of the neo-classical approach where share tenancy is explained as a device to stabilise family income, which is popularly known as the agricultural ladder hypothesis. This approach seems to have developed in the United States as a way of explaining share tenancy there (Winters, 1978). A strong adherent of this hypothesis, Robertson, following the Chyanovian line of thought argues that share tenancy is an arrangement to mitigate against the instability of the family as a productive unit and he defines:

Sharecropping is a means by which the process of production can be extended at a season's notice beyond the limits of the household, without violating its integrity as a unit of property holding and a consumption (Robertson, 1987).

Thus, the neo-classicists define share tenancy as a rational endeavour on the part of each of the parties involved to improve upon their initial welfare conditions. Here the socio-economic contexts in which the tenancy contracts are agreed upon are not taken into account. Economic rationality is isolated from the class dimension of a differentiated peasantry.

In contrast to this, Marx proceeds as follows:

"As a transitory form the original form of rent to capitalist rent, we may consider the metayer system, or share-cropping, under which the manager (farmer) furnishes labour (his own or another's), and also a portion of working capital, and the land lord furnishes, aside from land, another portion of working capital (e.g., cattle), and the product is divided between tenant and landlord in definite proportions which vary from country to country. On the one hand, the farmer here lacks sufficient capital required for complete capitalist management. On the other hand, the share here appropriated by the landlord does not bear the pure form of rent. It may actually include interest on the capital advanced by him and an excess rent. It may also absorb practically the entire surplus labour of the farmer, or leave him a greater or smaller portion of this surplus labour. But, essentially, rent no longer appears here as the normal form of surplus value in general. On the one hand, the sharecropper, whether he employs his own or another's labour, is to lay claim to a portion of the product not in his capacity as labourer, but as possessor of part off the instruments of labour, as his own capitalist. On the other hand, the landlord claims his share not exclusively on the basis of his landownership, but also as lender of capital" (Marx, 1974).

Here Marx considers sharecropping as a form of transitory rent and a method of surplus appropriation. Thus share tenancy is viewed as an intermediate form of rent between pre-capitalist ground rent in its pure form and capitalist rent. In contrast to the neo-classical definition of tenancy as an arrangement to increase static allocative efficiency, Marx considers tenancy in a dynamic context. Moreover, the terms and conditions of the contract are not determined at the individual level and on mutual agreement. Rather sharecropping is a class relation between landlord as the dominant class and the farmer as the subservient class. And sharecropping is not a technical arrangement to increase land productivity but a means of appropriating surplus. Thus neo-classical economists consider tenancy as essentially a contractual arrangement, whereas Marxists view it as essentially a production or class relation and a method of surplus appropriation.

Neo-classical analysis proceeds in terms of individual rationality whereas Marxists take into account the socio-economic matrix in which an individual is embedded. What neo-classical explain is choice after a feasible set has been determined. But, what is important and what they abstract from is how the feasible set is determined and who determines it? In other words who sets the rules of the game? While making a choice an individual has to see where he is and his position in the class hierarchy and what options are open to him out of which he has to choose. And here the prevailing power relation comes into play, which restricts the feasible choice of the weaker party in the transaction.

Bhaduri, an eminent Marxist theoretician, argues that class relations embody market relations and that exchange is a surface phenomenon of economic life, reflecting the underlying economic and social organization of production. His main contention is that in backward agriculture market forces are incipient and not adequately developed and that this inadequately developed market transactions is not triggered by the motive of gains from trade, but under compulsion of subsistence consumption needs which are to be met by entering into loan transactions with the dominant party. And this involuntary involvement in the market results in a cumulative process of forced commerce and unequal exchange by interlinking transactions in other markets like tenancy, produce, assets, labour and so on. Badhuri emphasizes that in backward agriculture, surplus extraction is in the nature of commercial exploitation and lies in the sphere of exchange rather than in production.

Bhaduri (1983) explains share tenancy as a form of *Labour process* and argues that the main intention of such a labour contract is to extract maximum amounts of man-hours of labour per acre leased out at a minimum of supervision cost under the threat of survival.

Thus the neo-classical definition of tenancy is contractual, while the Marxist interpretation of tenancy is one of surplus appropriation. One notes of the Marxist approach that it lacks a macro framework emphasizing clearly the macro variables that create favourable conditions for the landowning class, which this class then takes advantage of. The contingencies upon which the Marxist superstructure is to be built need to be carefully pointed out. More accurately, the macro variables, which limit the feasible choice, set of the landowning class or influence their enforcement device need to be recognised.

Tenancy and Efficiency

Share tenancy is often considered as a feature of feudalistic or pre-capitalist backward agriculture and is seen to be inefficient. Most of the early writers on share tenancy in the eighteenth and nineteenth centuries strongly condemned it. Thus to the Marquis of Mirabeau share tenancy was a "deplorable method of cultivation, the daughter of necessity and mother of misery".

But recently there has been a spurt of empirical work, which claims that share tenancy can be efficient and that it is a response to an imperfect world. With regard to the efficiency implication of tenancy the classical, neo-classical and Marxian writers hold different views. To avoid unnecessary sub-categories we join together the classical and neo-classical view under one head as their analytical framework is common.

Efficiency of Share Tenancy

Any discussion of the efficiency implication of sharecropping as an institution conveniently begins with Adam Smith. His interest lay in two central issues: the impact of product sharing on intensity of labour effort, and on farm investment. Smith argued that share tenancy provides some incentive to effort and that as a result labour productivity will increase as the labourer knows that part of the proceeds from the increased effort will accrue to him. But the tenant would be extremely reluctant to employ his own capital on the farm, as the landlord would receive a large part of the resultant product. In the words of Adam Smith (1969) "It could never, however be in the interest of (the metayer) to lay out, in the further improvement of the land, any part of the little stock which they might save from their own share of the produce, because the lord, who laid out nothing, was to get one-half of whatever is produced".

The attitude of the classical economists towards share tenancy was of disapproval and strong condemnation because of it acting as an effectual bar to agricultural progress.

The first formal statement concerning the allocative implication of sharecropping was presented by Marshall which has been known as the traditional, neo-classical or tax-equivalent approach. It is curious to note that until the time of Alfred Marshall, it was not clearly recognised that the argument which showed that the share tenant would under invest capital also sufficed to show that he would under supply work effort. In Marshall's own words "For when the cultivator has to give to his landlord half of the returns to each does of capital and labour that he applies to the land, it will not be to his interest to apply any doses the total return to which is less than twice enough to reward him. If, then, he is free to cultivate as he chooses, he will cultivate far less intensively than on the English plan; he will apply only so much capital and labour as will give him returns more than twice enough to repay himself so that his landlord will get a smaller share even of those returns than he would have on the plan of a fixed payment" (Marshall, 1961).

Thus according to Marshall under sharecropping total per hectare product and total per hectare land rent accruing to the landlord will be less than optimal. Though Marshall is often quoted as the chief architect of the inefficiency argument of share cropping, he himself very well knew that if the landowner possessed the opportunity to determine the inputs, which the tenant applies, then an efficient solution would result. This is quite clear when he writes, "if the control of the landlord is slight the cultivation is poor; but if it is effective the results may not be very different from those on the English plan". Marshal also eulogizes share cropping by suggesting that, "this plan has many of the advantages of the three modern systems of cooperation, profit sharing, and payment by piece-work".

But what worried Marshall was that under fixity of tenure as it existed in many parts of Europe, an efficient outcome depended on constant supervision and interference by the landlord. Marshall specifies the situations where share tenancy may be more efficient "the advantages of the metayer system are considerable when the holdings are very small, the tenants poor, and the landlords not averse to taking much trouble about small things: but that it is not suitable for holdings large enough to give scope to the enterprise of an able and responsible tenant". Thus Marshall was aware of the fact that most of the defects of share tenancy were a function of how it was practiced in a given context, and that there were conditions under which it could operate efficiently. Thus Marshall is erroneously associated with the inefficiency argument on share tenancy.

There are three techniques by which the landlord may enforce the desired intensity of cultivation by the tenant:

(a) By specifying in great detail what the tenant is required to do: cropping pattern, cultivation technique, labour input, fertilizer application and other input use;
(b) By sharing input costs in the same ratio as the crop share, i.e. cost sharing; and
(c) By granting short-term leases which makes possible periodic review of the performance of the tenant.

In addition to these three techniques, the landlord can impose an increased intensity of effort from the tenants who crucially depend on the meagre plot of leased land to earn their livelihood by leasing out land in small parcels to many poor tenants. Cheung (1969) accepted the first technique of enforcing the desired intensity of cultivation on the tenant and formalized it in his model. Newbery (1975) incorporated the second mechanism in his model.

However, Cheung was first formally to outline not only how sharecropping might be as productive as other forms of contract, but also the contexts in which it might be preferred contract. Cheung argues that "The implied resource allocation under private property rights is the same whether the landowner cultivates the land himself, hires farm lands to do the tilling, leases his holdings on a fixed rent basis, or shares the actual yield with his tenant." Cheung's model is often referred to as the "private property rights approach".

Cheung develops a model to demonstrate that with well-defined private property rights and free markets, resource allocation must be efficient, ragardless of the choice of tenancy. In his model the landowner's objective function is to maximise his wealth given his total land holdings subject to the constraint that the tenant gets his alternative earnings, i.e. his wage income. The control variables in the landlord's hand are the number of tenants among whom the given land holding will be parceled out, the rental percentage and the tenant inputs. Thus in Cheung's model the rental ratio is endogenously determined whereas the wage is given that will be achieved in a competitive wage labour market. Thus by assuming free and competitive market. Cheung completely ignored the overwhelming evidence that the choice of share tenancy is founded on the existence of fundamental market imperfections. Cheung treats rental share as the outcome of the landlord's profit maximisation exercise. In Cheung's model transaction cost is zero, therefore the landowner can monitor the tenant input level whereas in Marshall's model transaction cost is infinite as it is left to the tenant to decide its own input intensity.

The Marxist View: Share Tenancy as a Theory of Stagnation

Marxists consider the efficiency implication of share tenancy in a dynamic context. They argue that share tenancy is a remnant of feudalism and its persistence inhibits productive investment by diverting reinvestible surplus into unproductive channels like rack-renting, usury, trading etc. Thus share tenancy being a feature of agricultural backwardness also perpetuates underdevelopment and thus causes stagnation in agriculture. Views of eminent Marxists on the issue are discussed below.

Bhaduri's Model of Agricultural Backwardness

A distinguishing feature of the Smith-Marshall model of sharecropping is that the decision as to whether or not to invest or innovate is taken by the tenant, not by the landowner. In that model the landlord is passive, a sleeping partner, a pure renter, while the tenant exercises the role of a decision-maker. Recently an alternative model has been presented by Bhaduri (1973) in which the roles played by the sharecropper and landlord are reversed: the landlord is the active agent, in the sense that it is he who decides whether or not to innovate, while the tenant remains passive, becoming little more than an agricultural labourer paid in kind.

In Bhaduri's model the semifeudal landowner derives his income both from property right to land and usury. That is the landowner has two sources of income: (i) the rental income that he gets from the leased out land, and (ii) the interest that he charges for the loan advanced to tenants. If the landowner adopts technological innovation, the productivity will increase and consequently the crop income of the tenant will increase in absolute amount even if the share remains the same. Therefore, the tenant will borrow less to meet his consumption needs and the landowner will suffer losses in interest income. Therefore, the landlord will be discouraged from introducing any technological improvement so long as his gain in rental income from increased productivity brought by technological change falls short of his loss in income from usury due to a reduction in the level of consumption loan required by the farmer.

Bhaduri even argues that the semi-feudal landowner will resist big investments as it makes the tenant free from perpetual debt and destroys the political and economic control of the landowner on the tenant, even though on an exclusively economic ground it may be profitable to him. Thus, technological backwardness may be used as a control variable to reinforce existing asymmetry of economic power relations. A landowner may be inclined to adopt innovation, if he is benefited by it. But in order to promote his class efficiency and to maintain his economic power overtime, he will prefer not to invest. Thus, here maintenance of class efficiency in a dynamic context will distract him from adopting technical innovation.

But it has been argued by Newbery (1975) that if the landlord has sufficient power to withhold innovation, then he can extract the extra gain from the innovation by manipulating the rental share, the interest rates is questioned in the context of power relations that exist in backward agriculture as Bhaduri portrays them to be. But Bhaduri does not adequately explain the mechanism of the debt trap on which his theory rests squarely. That is, how does the indebtedness of the tenant persist and how is it an ongoing process in the village? Newbery clearly points out that the trap exists without the exercise of any power by the landlord. The peasant could free himself through his endeavour. A good year with a slightly better than usual harvest could set the peasant on his way to freedom. Therefore, the foundation of Bhaduri's thesis as a theory of stagnation is quite flimsy.

Patnaik's Argument: Existence of Pre-capitalist Rent as Barrier to Investment

Patnaik (1979), a leading exponent of Marxist ideas, argues that investing a given sum of money in direct capitalist cultivation in agriculture is conditional upon that sum of money yielding a surplus profit at least equal to the existing level of pre-capitalist rent over and above the average profit. Thus in a situation where capitalist production is confronted by existence of high level of pre-capitalist ground rent as a historically given conditions (as in India), this must also constitute a barrier to investment.

Bharadwaj's View: Diversion of Investible Surplus into Unproductive Channels

Bharadwaj (1985) has a broader framework than Patnaik as she takes into consideration the widespread existence of interlinked transactions where the landlord's income is not restricted to only rent. The landlord also advances loans at exorbitant interest rates to his tenants, and gets labour at less than the prevailing wage rate and buys crop produce at a predetermined lower price at the time of harvest. Therefore, the landlord's income is from a variety of sources and the aim is to extract maximum surplus from the deficit households.

Bharadwaj argues that the greater the predominance of chronically deficit households in the rural communities, the greater the diversion of re-investible resources into unproductive channels like usury, trading, labour attachment and tie-in-sales etc. Rural underdevelopment is thus attributed mainly to the existence of pre-capitalist mode of exchange, which acts as fetter on the development of productive forces and thereby reinforce the existing production relations. If the forces of productive accumulation, nurtured by a set of favourable initial conditions, generate a minimum pace, then they can succeed in breaking through the fetters of pre-capitalist remnants. In certain pockets like Punjab and Haryana where this has been achieved, there has come about capitalist accumulation and investment.

On the other hand, several economists argue that interlinkage cannot explain the rural backwardness as exists in today's South Asia, the reason to be sought somewhere else. Khasnabis's (1982) survey of tenurial arrangements in Nadia district of West Bengal reveals that no strong interlinkage could be found between tenancy contract and credit contract. A model of agrarian backwardness should therefore, to be based on some explanatory factors other than the interlinkage between credit conditions and tenurial arrangements. A non-legalised sharecropping arrangement that assures a high share of produce for the landowners wielding semi-feudal authority over the tenants in a near stagnant agrarian economy is the typical reality with respect to the observed households. No neat model on the lines of differential risk aversion, or varying bargaining power of individual lessors or lessees (Bharadwaj and Das, 1975) seems to be applicable to such an economy. An alternative analysis, mainly socio-political in nature, which discusses the process of interaction between the semi-feudal authority and the rural masses, might give a better insight into the problem.

But Lehman (1985) in his study of Ecuador argues that there does not seem to be any inherent incompatibility between sharecropping and capitalist development.

The increasing evidence of big farmers leasing in land and small farmers leasing out land in agriculturally advanced regions of India suggest that sharecropping does not in itself denote an exploitative relationship in which the lessor inevitably has the upper hand: he may be the impoverished victim of the contract and the tenant the prosperous capitalist.

Tenants are those who cultivate the land of others on payment of rent in cash or kind. The National Commission on Agriculture (1976) mentions the following categories of tenants:

(a) Tenants in the home farmlands of the ex-intermediaries
(b) Sub-tenants of the intermediaries
(c) Tenants holding lands from the riots in the riotwari areas
(d) Sharecroppers who are in most of the areas not included in the definition of the term 'tenant' though they have all the characteristic features of a tenant.

Tenancy reforms primarily aim at providing security of tenure and regulation of rent. The tenancy reforms laws make provisions for registering tenants, or giving ownership rights to the former tenants, to bring them directly under the state. States like Bihar, parts of Andhra Pradesh etc. have abolished tenancy altogether, while others like West Bengal have given clearly spelt out rights to recognized tenants and sharecroppers.

The implementation of these laws have led to only a small percentage of tenants acquiring ownership rights, but it has undoubtedly led to a sharp fall in the area under tenancy.

3. *Ceiling on Landholdings*

Ownership of land is subject to a limit under the land reform laws. Guidelines with regard to ceiling limit are as follows:

- The best category of land with assured irrigation and capable of yielding at least two crops a year should have a ceiling within the range of 4.05 to 7.28 acres, taking into account the fertility of the soil and other conditions.
- In the case of land having assured irrigation for only one crop in a year, the ceiling shall not exceed 10.93 acres.

- For all other types of land the ceiling shall not exceed 21.85 acres.
- The unit of application of ceiling shall be a family of five members, consisting of husband, wife and minor children. Where the number of members in the family exceeds five, additional land may be allowed for each member in such a manner that the total area admissible to the family does not exceed twice the ceiling limit for a family of five.
- Every major son will be treated as separate unit for the purpose of application of ceiling.
- Exemptions were to be allowed for plantations of crops like teà and coffee, Bhoodan Yagya Committees, registered cooperatives, and other bodies.

The actual ceiling as enacted by laws in the various states are given in the following Table:

Name of States	*Irrigated Two Crops Land (acres)*	*Irrigated One Crop Land (acres)*	*Dry Land (acres)*
Andhra Pradesh	4.05 to 7.28	6.07 to 10.93	14.16 to 21.85
Assam	6.74	6.74	6.74
Bihar	6.07 to 7.28	10.12	12.14 to 18.21
Gujrat	4.05 to 7.28	6.07 to 10.93	8.9 to 21.85
Haryana	7.25	10.9	21.8
Himachal Pradesh	4.05	6.7	12.14 to 28.33
Jammu & Kashmir	3.6 to 5.6	-	5.95 to 9.20*
Karnataka	4.5 to 8.10	10.12 to 12.14	21.85
Kerala	4.86 to 6.7	4.86 to 6.7	4.86 to 6.7
Madhya Pradesh	7.28	10.93	21.85
Maharashtra	7.28	10.93 to 14.57	21.85
Manipur	5.00	5.00	6.00
Orissa	4.05	6.7	12.41 to 18.21
Punjab	7.00	11.00	20.50
Rajasthan	7.28	10.93	21.85 to 70.82
Sikkim	5.06	-	20.23
Tamil Nadu	4.86	12.14	24.28
Tripura	4.00	4.00	12.00
Uttar Pradesh	7.30	10.95	18.25
West Bengal	5.00	-	7.00

The government of India notes that provisions like separate ceilings for major sons and exemptions for religious and charitable institutions, *benami* and *farzi* (types of practices to falsify land deeds) transfers are behind the wide gap between the expectation and performance of the ceiling laws. Other reasons include the generally poor quality of surplus lands and lack of financial and institutional support to bring these lands under cultivation.

When the question of redistribution of land came up, along with ceilings, it became necessary for the planners to recognize what minimum size these landholdings should be. The first Five Year Plan recognized an **economic holding** as one that affords a reasonable standard of living to the farmer and his family, providing full employment to a family of normal size and a pair of bullocks. A **basic holding** was defined as a holding smaller than an economic holding but larger than a holding which is palpably uneconomic on which individual farming would not be possible. A **family holding** was defined as three times the economic holding. Based on availability, landless families are allotted the equivalent of a family holding.

4. Consolidation of Landholdings

Consolidation refers to reorganization of fragmented holdings into one plot. Of all the land reform measures, this has received the least critical appreciation. The importance of consolidation and the ill effects of fragmentation must be understood. **Fragmentation** implies a stage in the evaluation of the agricultural holdings in which a single farm consists of numerous discrete parcels, often scattered over a large area. It results in inefficient use of soil, capital, and labour in the form of boundary lands and wasteful boundary disputes and litigation costs. It increases the difficulties of management and results in inadequate supervision. Efficiency of cultivation is considerably reduced, as a peasant family cannot manage widely divided plots. Fragmentation also prevents land improvement. Potential production increases due to land consolidation are estimated at as high as 25 per cent to 30 per cent. Unit cost decreases from 10 per cent to 15 per cent.

Resistance to land consolidation has come from the small and marginal landowners because of the fear of displacement among tenants and sharecroppers and lack of updated land records; the perceived advantage of having land in fragmented parcels in the event of floods and other natural calamities or acquisition for public purposes.

Among the many reasons, that consolidation is opposed by the peasantry the government notes the following:

- The apprehension that the bigger farmers will get a better deal, especially when land are not homogenous; and
- Strong local sentiments for attachment to land and inadequate participation and appreciation by the people.

5. Legislations and their Implementation

The state governments have tried to initiate these measures through legislation. Most of the major legislations those with far-reaching consequences, have been passed after 1947. In a total of 82 legislations enacted by the various States and Union Territories, about 30 (i.e. 36.6 per cent) deal with tenancy; in itself an indication of the importance given to the whole issue of tenants. The main features of the laws relating to land reforms are:

- All states initially passed laws to abolish intermediaries, with varying provisions for resumption for self-cultivation. The criteria for such resumption varied from state to state.
- Ceiling laws too showed wide variations in actual ceilings, strictures in implementation and dates of enactment of such laws.
- All laws provided heritable rights to the tenants. Eviction is possible only under circumstances of willful transgression of the conditions of lease, like permanently damaging the land, sub-letting, non-payment of rent or if the landowner wants the land back for self-cultivation.
- Provisions for redistribution in all states deem that SCs be given preference for allocation of surplus land.

- Provisions were made in every state with sizeable tribal populations to prevent land alienation from the tribals.

It is worth mentioning here that a greater number of laws passed in a state do not necessarily indicate the progress of land reforms as such in that state. For instance, West Bengal, one of the states where the efforts in land reform have been relatively commendable, has only two laws. It however includes all the important legislation related to land reforms. Implementing these laws, has however, been an uneven process in all the States. These differences were both in the timing of the laws as well as in their implementation.

Peasant Efforts

Peasant movements for agrarian reforms have always centred around the contentious issue of land ownership and/or distribution. Indeed, the very term 'peasant' has been defined to mean "tenant, sharecropper, small farmer not regularly employed, hired labour, and landless labourers". This definition, though narrow in range, serves to show the importance this class holds for any measures or movements connected with land reforms. Peasant proprietors, tenants and land labourers have risen in spontaneous protest over economic questions all through the British period, with limited results. Organized, successful movements of a politically aware peasantry have, however, taken place mainly in the twentieth century, with the notable exception of the Moplah rebellion of 1823 and the Deccan riots of 1829, both of which achieved some long-term results.

The twentieth century has seen some of the most violent and widespread peasant movements with far-reaching consequences. A lasting feature of peasant movements in this century as in the earlier one, is that they have always erupted in violent conflagrations between the two well-demarcated classes involved in land relations – those with land rights and those without, resulting often in violent police retaliation.

To present a comparable picture, the essential features, objectives and issues of some of these movements are compared in the Table below:

Movement	Causes	Focal Issues
Tebhaga, Bihar-Bengal, 1946	• Forcible collection of rent in spite of repeated famines. • Hoarding	The share of the landlord should be reduced to 1/3rd of the produce instead of ½.
Telangana, Andhra Pradesh, 1946-48	• Vetti (forced labour), • Impoverishment, • Growing indebtedness	Land to the tiller, abolition of vetti, and land redistribution.
Naxalbari, Bengal, 1967-70, West Bengal, Bihar, Andhra Pradesh	• Concentration of landholdings in spite of legislation. • Non-implementation of rights to protect tenants	Land to the tiller, through forced redistribution of lands and share in produce.

The main demands of these movements centered around reduction of excessive rent or revenue on produce and land redistribution from the rich to the poor. Many of the movements have provided the stimulus necessary for land legislation. Some of the major movements of this century are explained in brief below.

Peasant Movements in Bihar

Following the Champaran Satyagraha initiated by Mahatma Gandhi in 1917, Bihar became an important centre for peasant movements. Activities addressed solutions to the problems of sharecroppers, such as abolition of customary non-rent payments, regulation of eviction, and fixation of fair rent. The main centre of the movement was in north Bihar. The Bihar Kisan Sabha, which was started in 1927 developed into an extensive organization after 1934. Largely due to the efforts of Swami Sahajanand Saraswati, the Bihar Kisan Sabha was perhaps the strongest section of the All-India Kisan Sabha, which was subsequently formed.

With the passing of the Zamindari Abolition Act, 1949, the movements largely petered out. Post independent Bihar has seen an important land struggle in Bodhgaya starting in 1978. The peasants, under the leadership of the Yuva Chhatra Sangharsh Samity, organized a long drawn out struggle to secure land rights from the Shankar Math. The *mahants* (religious heads) of the Buddhist monasteries in the area had amassed huge amounts of land under the exemption given to religious and charitable institutions in the ceiling laws of the state. The peasants not only demanded that the land be legally registered in the names of the tillers, but also that women be given these rights. The situation erupted in violence as the *Mahants'* henchmen and police both tried to put down the movement. After the Supreme Court's directive to the effect that the land be handed over to the tillers, the struggle was considered to be successful. However, the initial objectives of giving land *pattas* to the women were not fulfilled in all except two villages.

Kisan Sabha and Khet Mazdoor Sabha in Uttar Pradesh

Kisan sabhas were started in some parts of Punjab, Bengal and U.P. in 1926-27. The main demands of the Kisan Sabha centred around problems of tenants, such as giving tenants occupancy rights, cancelling all rent arrears, reducing rent and water rates, abolishing non-rent extraction and forced labour.

The movement did not show much interest in agricultural labourers, leading to the establishment of the Khet Mazdoor Sabha in 1959. The demands of the tenants and of the agricultural workers were irreconcilable, so the latter initially restricted their demands to issues such as distribution of waste and surplus and government land, the disposition of land in surplus of the land ceiling regulation, and oppression of Harijans by the police and landlords, rather than issues such as increased wages or improved working conditions, which conflicted with the interests of the farmers.

Tebhaga Movement in Bengal

The All India Kisan Sabha had its political stronghold in the Bengal region. Despite repeated famines in the region, the tenants were still forced to surrender half of their produce to the landlords, evoked widespread dissent. The famine was worsened when the *Jotedar* (landlord) class, over the bodies of the famine-stricken, indulged in hoarding and black marketing in foodgrains as a way of amassing wealth. In 1946, the Sabha started the

Tebhaga movement, demanding that tenants be allowed to keep two-thirds of the produce. The main centres of the movement were in Dinajpur, Mymensingh and Susang, in present-day Bangladesh. One striking feature of the movement was the massive support it received from agricultural labourers. The main strategy of the agitation was to cut crops and remove the grain to the houses of the tenants without paying the landowner's share. The movement declined in 1947 due to crackdowns by the police, and the divisions that developed within the movement along religious lines.

Telangana Movement in Andhra Pradesh

The erstwhile State of Hyderabad, ruled by the Nizam of Hyderabad, was witnessed to one of the most politically effective peasant's movement of the century. The Tenangana region of present-day Andhra Pradesh was characterized by concentration of land ownership in the hands of very few ruling families, who oppressed the impoverished majority. The actual cultivators, who had no rights in the land that they had been tilling for generations, were subject to unjust treatment, high rent, growing indebtedness and a system of free labour known as the *vetti* system. The Communist Party of India took up these issues as the basis for a peasant's struggle against feudalism in the period 1946-48. Objectives of this armed struggle included land grabbing and redistribution, abolition of compulsory levy to the government, and stopping eviction of tenants under any pretext.

The struggle turned violent, forcing equally violent police retaliation against the Gram Raj Committees set up by the peasant groups to work as defence squads and institutions for self-governance.

As a result of this long drawn out struggle, the A.P. (Telangana Area) Tenancy and Agricultural Lands Act, 1950, was passed when the Indian Government took over from the Nizam's rule.

The lesson from Telangana was a dramatic demonstration of the importance of the peasant in any developing country in establishing political and economic stability.

Naxalbari Movement in West Bengal

In March 1967 the extremist faction of the communist

movement—the Communist Party of India (Marxist-Leninist) [CPI (ML)] started a liberation movement imitating one Chinese Model, in the village of Naxalbari, district Darjeeling in north Bengal. The basic issue of the movement was to secure rights to the marginalized sections of the agricultural community. In the course of the struggle, peasant committees were set up, land was redistributed, and landlords put on trial and executed. Village defense squads were established with agricultural labourers as its leaders. The middle and rich peasantry lent their support to the movement subsequently. The revolution was, however, quickly liquidated. A report published by the Ministry of Home Affairs in 1986 attributed the agrarian revolts connected with the Naxalite movement to the failure of the land reform programme.

The naxalbari movement is one of the most widespread movements of the present times. It no longer confines its issues to land reforms, but has widened its sphere of influence to the larger malaise of society-corruption, exploitation, maladministration. But the movement basically arose as a response to the dismal picture of land laws.

Voluntary Efforts

Traditionally, voluntary efforts in India have been basically concerned with educational and welfare-related activities to benefit the marginalised or disadvantaged sections of society. Gandhi's entry into the development scenario was the motivating factor, which led to the entry of much voluntary action groups in programmes for poverty alleviation. The initial voluntary efforts in this regard were made by these constructive programme organizations through promotion of village and cottage industries, animal husbandry and agriculture. It is only after the 1950s that the voluntary efforts started focusing on economic development programmes in a planned way. Following the failure of governmental policies to deal with the problem of poverty, voluntary efforts increasingly realized that welfare oriented activities will not be self-sustaining unless a direct effort is initiated to attack the background of economic backwardness. Subsequent international events focused even more sharply on the problems that afflict specific groups of the marginalized in society, viz. the poor, the disabled, women, children. Voluntary efforts too, accordingly, brought their agenda upto par with these changing national and international sensibilities by inculcating larger issues—poverty alleviation, income generation, watershed management, etc. Voluntary efforts can be broadly categorized under two heads: those initiated by individuals, and those by organizations, both formal and informal.

Individual Efforts

In pre-independent times, Gandhi initiated a focus on the rural disadvantaged, a traditional that was carried out by Vinoba Bhave to provide leadership to one of the most widespread consensus-based land reform programmes in the subcontinent i.e. the Bhoodan and Gramdan.

Bhoodan and Gramdan

The Bhoodan and Gramdan movements attempted to bring about what Vinoba Bhave called a "non-violent revolution" in India's land reforms programme. These integrated movements were an attempt to solve the land problem by urging the landed classes to voluntarily surrender a part of their land for the landless of the village.

On these, the Bhoodan was started earlier, in 1951. The problems faced by the landless *harijans* (a term used Gandhi to denote the ex-untouchables) were highlighted by the peasants themselves at one of Vinoba Bhave's regular prayer meetings being held at village Pochampalli in Telangana. In response to appeals by Vinoba Bhave to the landowning class in the village, some of them agreed to voluntary donate some portion of their lands to be redistributed to the landless of that village. This led to the birth of Bhoodan movement. A target was fixed for about 50 million acres of land to be available for redistribution through Bhoodan. Both the Central the State Governments provided the necessary assistance to Vinoba Bhave in fulfilling his mission.

Bhoodan gave way to the Gramdan movement, which came into being in 1952. The objective of the Gramdan movement was to persuade landowners and leaseholders in each concrete village to renounce their land rights, after which all the lands would become the property of a village association for egalitarian redistribution and joint cultivation. A village is declared as given in Gramdan when at least 75 per cent of its residents with 51 per cent of the land signify their approval in writing for Gramdan. The first village to come under *Gramdan,* was Magroth, district Haripur, Uttar Pradesh. It took more than three years to get another village as a gift.

By the mid-fifties, however, the movement received widespread political patronage. Government efforts aimed at Gramdan and Bhoodan as several laws were passed in the states. For instance Assam passed two laws—the Assam Gramdan Act, 1961, and the Assam Bhoodan Act, 1965. With its inculcation into the government programme, the quantity of land donated became more important than its quality. The movement reached their peak around 1969, by which time 86,709 villages had been declared as given in Gramdan. After 1969 Gramdan and Bhoodan lost its importance due to the shift from being a purely voluntary movement to a government-supported programme. All major political parties, seeking to gain mileage from this mass-based popular programme, incorporated the concepts of Bhoodan and Gramdan into their agenda. The shortcomings inherent in any government programme – red tapism etc. resulted in a dilution of the concept. After the withdrawal of Vinoba Bhave from the movement in 1967, it lost its mass base.

Of the total 42.6 lakh acres received through Bhoodan, 17.3 lakh acres were found to be unfit for cultivation. About 11.9 lakh acres were distributed and 13.4 lakh acres remained to be distributed. In the later period, landlords had mostly donated land under dispute or unfit for cultivation. Besides, the whole movement was treated as something apart from the general scheme of development rather than combining with the existing institutional means to try to make it a success. This separation from the mainstream scheme seriously affected both its continuances as a policy and effective implementation. However of all the attempts undertaken so far for the redistribution of land among the landless, Gramdan and Bhoodan are considered as the most effective, aiming at reducing the gap between the rich and the poor without resorting to any violence.

Organizational Efforts

The involvement of voluntary organizations and groups in poverty alleviation and land reform programmes has been comparatively recent. Between these two issues poverty alleviation had been taken up earlier. Land reforms as an issue, due to the political connotations attached to it, was by and large steered clear of by voluntary organizations other than those, which took up post-Bhoodan and Gramdan development programmes. Gandhian constructive organizations had initiated programmes aimed at poverty alleviation since pre-independent times. After the Bhoodan and Gramdan movements were started, many constructive organizations worked for the voluntary donation of land and its redistribution to the landless. However, land reform programmes were specifically added to the list of focal issues towards the end of the 1960s and beginning of 1970s, based on the realization that it is the core around which the whole issue of poverty removal and equality should revolve. The lack of administrative and political wills to make the governmental provisions a reality gave further impetus to the agenda of these organizations. Without land reforms, social tensions erupt in violent conflagrations, as was witnessed in the form of the Naxalite movement. The organizations could not shy from this vital issue if they were to set about trying to achieve their objectives. This realization was however confined to a minority, and did not gain general acceptance. This trend continues till date.

The organizations, which are involved in land reforms often, have multiple involvements in the land question. After the ceiling acts were implemented, acquiring land for redistribution was removed from the agenda issue for voluntary agencies. Instead, the agenda shifted to secure rights to the tenants and landless promoting the causes of land consolidation, identifying both beneficiaries for the programmes as well as landlords who are yet to be brought under the purview of ceiling, unearthing *benami* and *farzi* arrangements etc. Other than this, these activities mainly centres around the following areas:

(a) Generation of awareness among the peasants about the importance of the land reform and motivating them to initiate action against the violators of the laws. For instance, the Yuva Chhatra Sangharsh Vahini's activities in Bodhgaya wherein they tried to compel the *mahant* of the Bodh Gaya Math to part with the ceiling surplus land under his control.

(b) Distribution of *pattas* among the landless allottees, who have not been given formal ownership rights on paper. The activities of Banwasi Seva Ashram (Sonebhadra, Uttar Pradesh); Tribal Development Training Institute (Ambikapur, Madhya Pradesh); Anand Niketan Ashram (Baroda, Gujarat); Edta Parishad (Madhya Pradesh); Shram Bharati (Munger, Bihar) are some instances of activities undertaken in this direction.

(c) Provision of legal assistance and guidance to the rural poor to deal with the legalities of land rights. Organizations that work on distribution of *pattas* also deal with providing assistance on the legal angle, as these issues are often interlinked.

(d) Identification of the landless for purposes of redistribution of surplus land.

(e) Provision of training in agriculture and supplying of inputs—seeds, fertilizers, technology appropriate for small farms, equipment. Some of these organizations are: Water Development Society (Rohtas, Bihar); Gujarat Institute of Area Planning (Bedchi, Gujarat); Tamulpur Anchalik Seva Sangh (Kamrup, Assam); Tagore Society for Rural Development (West Bengal); and Sarva Seva Sangh Farm (Tamil Nadu).

(f) Organization of cooperatives and training in collective farming. Institute for Motivating Self-Employment (Calcutta, West Bengal), Organization of the Poor (Ghazipur, Uttar Pradesh); Gram Lok Seva Sangh (Kamrup, Assam).

(g) Programmes like Socio-Economic Development Programme are focusing on the environmental concerns connected with land. This programme, for instance, is engaged in programmes of soil conservation and control of salinity, improvement of fisheries, healthcare, etc. In the field of land reform it helps the rural poor by informing about land reform measures, assisting labourers to get land for cultivation on sharecropping basis, and by encouraging cooperative farming.

The organizations specifically work through people's groups, called *Lok Samitys, Gram Sabhas,* or People's Committees. The organisation of such activities is not a smooth affair. Organisations that do get involved in direct confrontations with the question of land redistribution often acquire political overtones later in their lifetime. They are often faced with opposition from vested interests both in the government and outside it. Such opposition often takes the form of physical assaults, character assassinations, etc. Despite these problems, the organizations have been able to effectively play their role in efforts at redistribution, providing *pattas* and thereby ensuring ownership rights and thereby protecting them from exploitation; besides providing training, infrastructure, and credit at both individual and collective levels.

Combined Efforts

Innovative ways to deal with the land problem are rare. However, wherever the government has tried to initiate or implement a programme with the active cooperation of the peasants, such efforts have largely been successful.

Present Database

Land, Land Tenures etc. are under the exclusive legislative and administrative jurisdiction of the states as provided in Entry No. 18 of List II (State List) of the Seventh Schedule to the Constitution. However, the Central Government has been playing an advisory and coordinating role in the field of land reforms since the First Five Year Plan. Agrarian reforms have been a core issue for Rural Reconstruction as a means of ensuring social justice to actual tillers and the landless rural poor, thereby creating a sustainable base for the overall growth of the industrial and tertiary sectors of our economy. Generating greater access to landless rural poor to land is considered an important component of poverty alleviation.

The Department of Land Resources under the Ministry of Rural Development has, therefore, been playing a crucial role in evolving a national consensus for initiating effective land reforms. The Department also initiated amendments of the Constitution 13 times for incorporation of 277 land laws in the Ninth Schedule to the Constitution. The last amendment was the 78th Amendment of the Constitution to incorporate 27 land laws in the Schedule.

The Land Reforms Division in the Department of Land Resources also acts as the nodal division of the Ministry of Rural Development for administration of the Land Acquisition Act, 1894, including issues covered under Entry No. 42 of the Concurrent List of the Seventh Schedule to the Constitution.

Under the major Land Reforms Activities actual achievements could be presented with the following tables under each important activities:

A. Conferment of Ownership Rights to Tenants

State	*No. of tenants (in Lakhs)*	*Area Accrued (in Lakh Acres)*
West Bengal	14.60	Not Reported
INDIA	124.22	156.30

Source: Annual Report 2003-2004, Government of India, Ministry of Rural Development.

B. Distribution of Surplus Land

State	*Area declared surplus (acres)*	*Area taken possession (acres)*	*Area distributed to individual beneficiaries (acres)*	*Total no. of beneficiaries*
West Bengal	1388506	1298892	990511	2680666
INDIA	7336195	6481247	5293679	5673103

Source: Annual Report 2003-2004, Government of India, Ministry of Rural Development.

State	Total no. of beneficiaries	SC		ST		Others		Not distributed (acres)	Under litigation (acres)
		No.	Area (acres)	No.	Area (acres)	No.	Area (acres)		
West Bengal	2680666	994220	370740	516536	223423	1169910	396348	315043	188887
INDIA	5673103	2041027	1799074	834728	780563	2797348	2714042	1162632	848951

Source: Annual Report 2003-2004, Government of India, Ministry of Rural Development.

C. Distribution of Bhoodan Land

State	*Area (Lakh Acres)*		
	Donated	*Distributed*	*Balance*
West Bengal	Negligible	Negligible	Negligible
INDIA	39.16	21.75	17.41

Source: Annual Report 2003-2004, Government of India, Ministry of Rural Development.

D. Distribution of Government Waste Lands

State	*Distributed in Lakh Acres*
West Bengal	4.32
INDIA	147.47

Source: Annual Report 2003-2004, Government of India, Ministry of Rural Development.

E. Consolidation of Holdings

State	*Area in Lakh Acres*
West Bengal	Not Available
INDIA	1633.47

Source: Annual Report 2003-2004, Government of India, Ministry of Rural Development.

2

Tenancy Reforms in West Bengal

Land relations, by their very nature, are embedded in the specificity of the history of a country or a region. Therefore, a proper evaluation of contemporary changes demands brief review of the evolution of land relations in a historical perspective. However, no more than a broad outline can be presented here.

Tenancy Reforms in the Pre-British Period

In Pre-British India, the ruling powers generally collected a portion of produce as land revenue. However, despite immense variations in the conditions of production or the quantum of revenue, both over regions and in time, the cultivation peasants in general appeared to have enjoyed some traditional and customary rights over the lands, which they occupied.

Historians have estimated the land revenue in different periods of ancient and medieval India as having varied from 1/12 to 1/3 of the produce. As regards the rights of cultivators, two sorts of rights were generally recognised since the thirteenth century: those of the *khudkasht* cultivators enjoyed all the customary rights including the right of undisturbed possession so long as they paid their due rent. The *pahikasht,* however, were not immuned from the hazards of eviction.

The first imperial land revenue settlement was introduced in Bengal during the reign of Akbar (1556-1605). The state demand was generally fixed at the level of 1/3 of the gross produce. As far as possible, settlement was made directly with the cultivators. The cultivators were given option of paying the revenue either in cash or in kind but the imperial preference for each payment was made explicit.

Tenancy Reforms in the British Period

When the East India Company obtained the rights of *diwani* (revenue administration) over Bengal in 1765, their attempts to collect revenue caused considerable disruption and disarray. The Company made arbitrary changes in the existing revenue system ignoring all customary rights and the minimum requirements of the people of the area. They tried first a quinquennial settlement (1772) and then a decennial settlement (1789). It can be reasonably argued that these two settlements were the harbingers of the more important Permanent Settlement of 1793.

In the period preceding Permanent Settlement, the Board of Directors of the Company made a few experiments, the most important of which was the introduction of Revenue Farm Contracts on a 5-yearly basis. Revenue collecting rights were given by auction to the highest bidders for a period of 5 years at a time. This system naturally led to extreme rack-renting and forcible collection and placed an unbearable burden on the cultivating peasantry.

Before the introduction of the Permanent Settlement, the following categories of landlords existed in the province of Bengal- (i) The old independent chiefs, like the Rajas of Cooch Behar, parts of Assam, Tripura etc., who retained their territories by paying tributes to the imperial power in Delhi. (ii) The old-established landlords (*bhuswamis*) who were *de facto* rulers of their estates and regions, such as the *Rajas* of Burdwan and Dinajpur. (iii) Collectors of revenue inducted by Mughal rulers whose rights became hereditary. (iv) Revenue Farmers who were in charge of revenue collection, while managing areas under their own possession. The permanent settlement at one stroke levelled all these categories and brought them under a single category, i.e., zamindars. This meant loss of privilege for some and elevation into privilege for others.

At the time of Permanent Settlement

A major economic logic behind the Permanent Settlement lay in the attempt by the British rulers to secure a stable state share as the first charge on the land. It has already been pointed out that by 1765 the East India Company acquired monopoly rights of revenue of collection from a large part of Eastern India, namely the then Bengal Presidency comprising Bengal, Bihar and Orissa. Economic historians have suggested that there was a pressure for increasing revenue collection from these regions because of the bullion control measures adopted by the Government in England. To enable the Company in India, to finance the collection of locally manufactured products for export to Europe, and to meet the vastly increased military expenditure (concomitant to the policy of annexation and expansion into other areas of the subcontinent) the Company needed more revenue. This is what was then known as the Investment Policy of the Company. The Pre-Permanent Settlement arrangements proved disastrous. Unbridled extortion on the one hand created considerable unrest and on the other brought in its train the famine of 1770. This led the British policy makers to opt for more durable settlement.

The Permanent Settlement was introduced in 1793. The State, in this case the British ruling power in India, assumed supreme rights over the land. The zamindars were made the agents of the state for the principal purpose of depositing to the treasury the annual revenue fixed in perpetuity for each estate. In return, the zamindars were given proprietary rights over their estates, which they could buy and sell, and the right to obtain rents from their tenants. Initially, however, there was a declaration of pious wish that there would be a concomitant fixation of rent on a permanent basis forth the cultivators too, but this was soon given up.

The provisions of the Permanent Settlement give no protection to either subordinate intermediaries or the cultivating tenants. In fact, the customary rights that the tenants had enjoyed almost without intermediaries, i.e., the zamindars, were for the first time in India made virtually permanent and hereditary proprietors of the land and their estates became marketable commodities. In the body of enactment there was no provision constraining this proprietary right of the zamindar in order to protect the customary rights of the cultivating peasants.

In the conditions created by the colonial of the nineteenth century, most of the proprietors, instead of managing the estates directly and undertaking the responsibility of improving the conditions of land and agriculture, embarked on a system of subinfeudation. The chain of subinfeudation resulted in a tremendous increase in the rental burden on the actual tillers of the soil. Even in cases where there was no subinfeudation, the cultivators were rack-rented and the local officials, the *naibs* (agents of absentee zamindars), became de facto zamindars and oppressed cultivators by imposing innumerable kinds of illegal exactions. The basic anti-cultivator and pro-landlord character of the settlement was greatly reinforced by two further regulations: the introduction of the Regulation VII of 1799 (known as *Haptam*) and Regulation V of 1812 (known as *Pancham*). These two regulations allowed the landlords practically unrestricted authority of seizing the crops and other personal property of the cultivators and to arrest them physically for realising rent arrears. This resulted in a virtual reign of terror and unbearable misery for the tenantry. Eviction of ryots became rampant after the enactment of these two regulations. It is possible that this period saw a significant rise in the proportion of landless cultivators in the rural areas of eastern India.

Tenancy Legislation after the Permanent Settlement

The main aims of the Permanent Settlement: (i) steady and substantial revenue, (ii) improvement of law and order, and (iii) undisturbed husbanding of land and an agriculture capable of meeting the minimum requirements of the cultivators over and above revenue and rent demands were not achieved. On the contrary, the unrestricted power of landlords and complete denial of the customary rights of the native tenantry created conditions of growing unrest. The period after the Permanent Settlement saw peasant protests all over the region. But it took more than half a century for the alien rulers to officially react to the situation and attempt minimal legal restrictions on the powers of the landlords oppressing the peasantry.

Rent Act of 1859

The Act of 1859 was the first tenancy legislation after 1793 that was meant to improve the relations between the landlords and their tenants. Its avowed purpose was to strengthen the position of the ryots *vis-à-vis* the landlords through a definition of the formers' rights as also to restrict the landlords' powers of arbitrary rent enhancement and eviction. The Act amended the law of distant (the Haptam) and abolished the zamindar's power to compel the ryots to report of the estate offices where they were often subjected to torture and intimidation.

The provisions of protection against rent enhancement and eviction related to only two categories of ryots. Firstly, a small group known as, *mukararidars* or *intamararidars* were entitled to hold land at rates fixed from the time of Permanent Settlement. Secondly, occupancy ryots, i.e., ryots who had cultivated or held land for a period of 12 years, were declared as provision that heritable occupancy right would not apply in cases of *khamar, nij jot* or *sir* land of the landlords. There were other restrictive clauses.

Another important feature of the Rent Act of 1859 was that it conferred on occupancy ryots the unhindered right of subletting. Thus it is the Rent Act of 1859 that acted as the fountainhead for the creation of a long chain of legalized subtenancy along with a large spill over area of unrecognised subtenancy in the form of share tenancy, mainly in the areas enjoying protection from the application of Rent Act.

It is in the above context that the Rent Law Commission was appointed by the Government of India in 1879 to prepare a digest of the existing laws and to draw a consolidated enactment. This culminated in the famous Bengal Tenancy Act of 1859.

Bengal Tenancy Act of 1885

The Bengal Tenancy Act (BTA) of 1885 recast the provisions of the earlier Act of 1859, more elaborately categorised the tenants, provided for incidence of different categories of tenants and their liabilities, put restrictions on arbitrary enhancement of rents, provided for special provisions regarding questions of the rights of the settled ryots. It made some special provisions regarding the contract between landlords and tenants. This Act for the first time provided a separate chapter on the rights of the tribals inhabiting the then providence of Bengal. In section 89 of this Act it was provided that no ejectment was permissible without an execution of a decree from the civil court. The Act also, from the first time, provided for the preparation of a record of rights and settlement of land revenue. The restrictions on the power of eviction put some restraint on the landlords and provided some relief to different categories of ryots having varying degrees of occupancy rights.

According to the BTA of 1885 landlords were allowed to retain their property rights as intermediaries. Their right to alienate the intermediary interests continued to exist but not the earlier powers of eviction or infringement of the rights of the incumbent tenants. The Act, however, allowed the landlord the right of resumption, an instrument by which eviction would be possible. The Act of 1885 made no attempt to link up owing occupancy rights to lease out their land to cultivators without any legal rights of occupation. Sharecroppers as a category did appear in the list of tenants and subtenants enumerated in the BTA, but while the Act defined the obligations of the sharecroppers, it remained ambiguous in respect of their rights.

BTA Amendments

The period between 1928 and 1940 witnessed several successive amendments to the provisions of Bengal Tenancy Act. The major amendments came in 1928, 1938, 1939 and 1940. The 1928 amendment extended the anti-eviction provisions of the BTA in favour of the ryots to the level of non-occupancy ryots and under-ryots. Consequent to the granting of some ryots in the occupancy ryots in the BTA of 1885, the number of non-occupancy ryots and under-ryots increased manifold in the following period. The 1928 amendment provided for restrictions on the eviction of under-ryots and on rent augmentation practiced by landlords in case of non-occupancy ryots. It may not be irrelevant here to point out that eviction and subsequent new settlement was the major instrument that was used by landlords for the enhancement of rent and making extortionate demands over and above the legal rent from the peasantry. In this respect, the 1928 amendments did represent some advance in protecting the ryots and under-ryots. However, such a legalistic regulation of the rights of the tenantry demanded a formal definition of ryots within the existing legal framework. In practice this meant that sharecroppers were not legally recognised as ryots.

Thus while the amendments of 1928 did register some advance for a section of the tenantry, it represented a definite retrograde step in the case of sharecroppers. During the period between 1885 and 1928, and more specifically between 1900 and 1920, officers engaged in settlement work did often record the incidence of sharecropping while preparing the record of rights in accordance with the provisions of BTA.

The land legislation and tenancy reforms by the colonial state before and after 1793 failed miserably in preventing the deteriorating toiling peasantry in particular. Its supposed intentions of not disturbing the traditional and customary rights prevailing in the country and its attempts at the same time to guarantee a secure base for revenue extraction and commercial exploitation of the countryside proved disastrous.

The Situation before 1947

As already mentioned the BTA and its amendments till 1935 failed to a large extent to remove the oppression and misery of the peasantry. This was the basis on which, from the 1920s and particularly after the 1930s, political mobilisation of the peasantry started. On the one hand, it is the genius of a leader like Mahatma Gandhi that enabled the Congress movement to reach out to the broad masses of peasants in the country and placed the peasantry of India within the political map of the country. On the other, concurrently, the nascent left forces started organizing the toiling peasantry on class lines through organisations like the *Kisan Sabha, Krishak Samity* etc., to struggle against not only the alien rulers but also the big landlords and tenure-holding jotedars. The rising forwent in the rural areas had to be taken into cognizance by the British government in India. It yielded to the setting up a new Land Revenue Commission under the Chairmanship of Sir Francis Floud, for a thorough and comprehensive review of the land revenue system. The commission submitted its report in 1940. The most important recommendations of this Commission may be presented as follows:

1. Acquisition of all rent-receiving interests on payment of compensation.
2. Tenancy rights to bargadars on a fair rent. And until the eventual abolition of bargadari, modification of share terms of 50 : 50 into 66 : 33 in favour of the bargadars.
3. Introduction of an agricultural income tax.
4. Prohibition of all subletting.
5. Desirability of ceiling on land holdings.

These recommendations, as can seen, did provide a rational approach for a restructuring of socio-economic relations in the rural areas and acted as a model for subsequent reforms. But these recommendations were not put into effect immediately.

Meanwhile, the Fazlul Haq Ministry (which enjoyed the support of the peasantry of Bengal in general, and the toiling Muslim peasantry of Eastern Bengal in particular) introduced the Agricultural Debtor's Act, 1933 and the Moneylenders' Bill in 1939 and relieved the debt burden of the suffering peasantry to a considerable extent. There amendments, made between 1938 and 1940, resulted in:

1. Permanency of occupation and right of alienation for all levels of the recognised tenantry, and
2. Rent, for all practical purposes, being frozen for all levels of tenancy.

Land Legislation in Post-Independence Period

The first enactment relating to land in the Post-Independence period was the West Bengal Non-Agricultural Tenancy Act, 1949. This act regulated the rights and interests of non-agricultural tenants and under-tenants.

Next came the Bargadari Act of 1950. This act, for the first time after the Bengal Tenancy Act (1985), recognised sharecroppers as some kind of legal under tenants and eligible to justifiable rights and responsibilities. It may be worth noteing here that during December 1946 to January 1947, a draft bill relating to the rights of bargadars was circulated by the then Muslim League Ministry of H.S. Suhrawardy, presumably in direct response to the *Tebhaga* movement then sweeping large parts of peasant Bengal. This draft Bill, however, was withdrawn in view of the final transfer of power and the attending partition negotiations (1947) coming to a decisive phase. The 1950 Bargadari Act was to a large extent similar to the earlier draft of 1946-47.

The Bargadari Act of 1950 recommended a 60 : 40 share in favour of such sharecroppers who were supplying the means of production line seeds and manure. But it did not provide for the protection of sharecroppers from possible eviction. Further, there was no provision for compulsory recording of sharecropping rights. Given these shortcomings effective implementation of the Act was out of the question.

In fact, while on a general plans the Bargadari Act, 1950 did herald the period of growing legislative attention to the problem of bargadars, its immediate practical effect was to provoke a large-scale eviction of bargadars by landowners from their traditional possessions. All records admit the eviction of bargadars on an unprecedented scale in the early 1960s.

The more important legislation was the West Bengal Estates Acquisition Act (WBEAA) of 1954. The Bill for enactment was introduced in May 1953 and became effective in February 1954, after receiving the Presidential assent required for such legislation. This Act was framed in the light of the opinions of the Land Revenue Commission and the committees set up subsequently.

The WBEAA was conceived primarily as a legislation for the abolition of the intermediary interests in land and finally doing away with the skeleton of the Permanent Settlement of 1793. It needs to be pointed out here that legislation subsequent to 1793, especially since 1885, considerably modified the original Settlement. Eviction of ryots and enhancement of zamindari rental demands, the two main instruments of oppression against the ryot title-holders, had been largely blunted even before the transfer of power. But the problems of under-tenancy in general and sharecropping tenancy in particular became more important.

The avowed purposes of the WBEAA of 1954 were as follows:

1. To eliminate the interests of zamindars and other intermediaries by acquisition and payment of compensation.
2. Restriction of *Khas* (demesne) holdings to stipulated limit (ceiling) and the recognition of such (intermediaries) holders as direct tenants under the state in respect to their below ceiling *khas* holdings.
3. Acquisition of all zamindari and other intermediary interests in mines, minerals, markets, forests, fisheries, etc.

The original Act was by 1955 amended and a provision for a ceiling on individual holdings of large landowners, irrespective of the nature of their titles, was incorporated.

The implementation of the WBEAA (1954-55) necessitated the preparation of a record of rights and this initiated the so-called Revisionary Settlement (R.S. 1956) and it is during this period that landowners and intermediaries showed great ingenuity in stalling effective implementation of the Act. The vested interests in land went to great lengths in creating false transfers (*benam*). Maximum use was made of the loopholes in the law by legal and extra-legal means. Thousands of acres were illegally retained; fictitious charitable trusts and endowments were created. Arable lands were converted into lakes, fisheries and orchards.

In the face of the tremendous offensive launched by the vested interests in land through such means, the affected peasantry was helpless. But by about the beginning of 1960s active resistance by bargadars against eviction started gaining momentum. The Estates Acquisition Act was later incorporated in the more comprehensive Land Reform Act of 1955. Further amendments were made subsequently. There was an amendment in the bargadari aspect: in 1956 a provision for an instrument called the *Bhagchas* Board (Sharecropping Adjudication) was added. It was recommended that the bargadars incumbent on land above the ceilings should be automatically deemed as direct tenants. Clauses for exemptions on grounds of personal cultivation were made marginally more restrictive. There were further amendments: in 1965 in respect of transfers of holdings; and in 1971 for augmenting the share of the sharecroppers form 60 : 40 to 75 : 25. In 1975, amendments were made for homestead land acquisition. Finally came the West Bengal Landholding Revenue Act, 1979 and the Revenue Rules of 1980. The 1979 amendment should be considered as a radical departure in clinching the issue of bargadari settlement on a juridical basis. The three most outstanding features in this respect provided for in the 1979 amendments are the following:

1. The responsibility of disproving a claim to bargadari rights was squarely put on the landowners.
2. Personal cultivation was defined as, "cultivation on the basis of physical participation by the members of the landowners' family".
3. A stringent residential clause, stipulating residence of the claimant to resumption within a distance of five miles from the plot of land claimed, was introduced.

These three features together decisively tilted the judicial provisions in favour of the practicing bargadars.

Operation Barga

Operation Barga is no new legislation. The Left Front Government came to power with an effective majority in 1977. In view of its experiences during two earlier shorter terms (1967 and 1969), the Front took seriously the implementation of the land reform measures already enacted during the last two decades. What is novel about Operation Barga is that the drive to register the names of sharecroppers (to ensure their legal rights) is undertaken with the active assistance of not only the bargadars themselves but also of rural workers' organisations and self-governing institutions. Operation Barga, launched by the end of 1978, directs land reform officials to conduct group meetings with the potential beneficiaries. Tentative lists of bargadars are prepared after such meetings and published for verification on the next day. After the field verification, a provisional list is hung up at all important places in the villages. Landowners are given the opportunity to file objections, which are also heard and verified, in the field in public. Thereafter, certificates of sharecropping are distributed among the beneficiaries. This method (Operation Barga), which depends heavily on group action by sharecroppers, is qualitatively different from the traditional revenue court approach, which by its very procedures, was tilted in favour of the landowners.

Operation Barga: Historical Background

Pre-Independece Period

From the very ancient times cultivation of land has been carried out not only by the owner of the land, but also by other persons employed by the owners. These could be slaves or wage labourers paid in kind or cash. The labourers who were given a share of the produce also did cultivation of land. The system of cultivation emerged in different forms not only in Bengal or in India but also throughout the world to suit the requirement of thethen rural society. The more uncertain was the agricultural production, the more were the possibilities of having share-tenancy system of cultivation.

A careful probe into the history of the land tenure system in India reveals that during the Buddhist, Hindu and Mughal periods share cropping in some form or other was not unknown. In some pockets of India some of the agricultural labourers during these periods were given a share of the produce in exchange of their labour.

During the British period, the land policies adopted by the British Administration made a crucial impact on the over-all agrarian system of India, especially in Bengal. Their prime objective was to raise more revenue through different types of experiments on the agrarian system in India. The East India Company created the Zamindari system to collect as much revenue as possible through Zamindars. Zamindari contract was given to the highest bidder. The famine of 1770 had crushed the financial position to the Zamindars as they failed to collect revenue from their tenants. At that time the British rulers introduced for Bengal a five-year (*Panchsala Bandobasto*) Settlement in 1772, but this quinquennial farming settlement had never been successful and it was replaced by the decennial settlement in 1786. The decennial settlement was subsequently declared permanent in 1793. It was the major turning point in the history of land relations of Bengal.

The Permanent Settlement of revenue with Zamindars was made the agents of the state and was responsible to deposit annual revenue for their concerned 'Estate' to the treasury. In return, the Zamindars were allowed to convert uncultivated barren lands into agricultural land to collect a share of the produce or a fixed rent on these lands for which the company did not claim additional revenue.

In the permanent Settlement, the rayots or even the subordinate intermediaries though they were not given any legal protection, being the agents of the '*de facto*' zamindars exploited the cultivators by imposing many kind of illegal economic burdens on them. This anti-cultivator character of the 'Permanent Settlement' was further strengthened by two other regulations e.g. 'Haptam' (regulation VII of 1799) and 'Pancham' (regulation V of 1812).

These repressive measures in the post permanent settlement period were followed by a large number of peasants uprising and protest. The colonial power noticed the instability in rural Bengal and tried to redress the situation to stabilise their rule and ensure their profits. The British gave some kind of legal protection to a section of peasants through the Rent Act of 1859 and later through the Bengal Tenancy Act of 1885. In the Rent Act of 1859 the occupancy rayots were free to sublet their lands. Consequently, this Act created a long chain of different forms of sub-tenancy, including share-tenancy. The Bengal Tenancy Act of 1885 specified that no ejection was permissible without a decree from the civil court. This restriction on the power to evict tenants put some kind of check on the landlord. However the landlords were allowed by the Act to evict tenants on the plea of the right of resumption. Moreover, the act did not try to linkup occupancy rights with the actual tillers of the soil. So the occupancy rayots gave the right to lease out their land to the actual cultivators who did not have any legal occupancy rights, but remained tenants-at-will.

In the words of the National Commission of Agriculture, "The Bengal Tenancy Act of 1885 conferred no rights on Bargadars or share croppers who constituted the great bulk of tillers of the soil and who remained tenants-at-will subject to arbitrary eviction and rack renting".

The National Commission observed that the Bengal Tenancy Act of 1885 as amended in 1928 and then again in 1933, gave protection to the upper strata of the rayots, who represented the middle elements of rural society between the landlords and the cultivating peasants.

"The rayots who actually took advantage of that Act were generally speaking, influential persons with substantial holdings." The Commission pointed to the fact that "most of them did not cultivate land by themselves but rented in out to Bargadars." And in the opinion of the Commission "the Tenancy act of 1885 in Bengal did not even touch the cringe of the problem of the disinherited and oppressed peasantry and sharecroppers created by the zamindari .... tenure system."

Sub-tenant or under rayots paying fixed rent on some recognition and subsequently enjoyed some rights or tenancy since 1885. But the sub-tenant under crop sharing system remained totally neglected. And over time, the extent or areas under sharecropping and number of sharecroppers increased significantly.

Introducing of the Permanent Settlement followed up by the above mentioned Act and also with the creation of white collar job opportunities in urban areas gave way for the mushroom growth of under-tenants having no legal rights on land, most of whom were bargadars or sharecroppers.

Post-Independence Period

In the post-independence period a series of land reform measures were undertaken by the government to cope with the uneven land distribution and repressive bargadary systems. The first post-independence legislation in favour of the bargadars in West Bengal was the 'Bargadary Act of 1950'. In this Act the bargadars were recognised as some kind of legal under-tenant. This Act recommended a 60 : 40 share in favour of such bargadars who would be responsible for supplying manual labours, draught animals/power, seeds and manure. The landowner on the pretext of 'personal cultivation' could evict bargadars from his land. This Act indirectly provoked many landowners to evict their bargadars from their traditional possessions. At that time the West Bengal Estate Acquisition Act (WBEAA), 1954 was promulgated. The primary motive of this Act was to abolish all intermediary rights on land, which the Zamindars were enjoying from the period of permanent settlement in 1793. The West Bengal, Land Reforms Act, 1955 repealed the Act of 1950. In the West Bengal Tenancy Act of 1956, provisions were made to protect the occupancy rights of the bagradars. But in the face of the oppressive and offensive measures launched by the land owning group a large number of sharecroppers were evicted. The West Bengal Land Reforms Act 1955, with its amendments from time to time, mainly deals with the provisions for (i) protecting the rights of share-croppers; (ii) the determination of the relative share of total produce to be paid by the bargadars; and (iii) conditions for termination of cultivation on barga land. In this Act, legal power was given to the officers to deal with the above mentioned matters and other related disputes in connection with '*Bhagchas*' (crop sharing). In actual practice the poor share coppers were helpless and failed to get the benefits of this Act. In 1965 amendment of Land Reforms Act, some provisions relating to shares were made, but this Act also failed to give adequate benefit to the sharecroppers. In order to protect the interests of the bagradars the following restrictions were imposed by the Act, in a situation where the landowner will be entitled to terminate cultivation by a bargadar:

- If a bargadar fails to cultivate the Land or uses it for other than cultivation purpose,
- If a bargadar does not cultivate the land personally,
- If the bargadar fails to tender the due share of the produce to the land owner, and
- If the landowner require the land for bringing it under personal cultivation.

Again an amendment of the Bargadar Act was made in 1971-72 to enhance the share of the sharecropper from 60 : 40 to 75 : 25. In this Act there is a provision that a landowner can't simply evict a bargadar on the plea of bringing the land under personal cultivation. The restrictions imposed are as follows:

I. A landowner cannot evict his bargadar for his personal cultivation if his total land under personal cultivation exceeds three hectares.
II. The landowner is not entitled to evict a sharecropper if by such termination the total land cultivated by a bargadar is reduced to less than one hectare. However, a bargadar under this Act may be evicted if he cultivated, and in excess of six hectares.

Those acts especially Bargadar Act, 1972 was no doubt radical for safeguarding the interests of the bargdars. But due to lack of effective implementation of the measures, on the one hand and vigorous offensive measures, undertaken by the landowner against the bargadars on the other, the provisions of the Act were of little use to the bargadars. The bargadars also had no easy access to the *Bhagchas* office or civil court. Consequently the peasant movement became intensive.

This movement with the slogan 'Land to the tillers and no eviction will be allowed' caught the attention of the intellectuals and politicians. The left parties began to organise many movements against the then ruling party. When the 'Left-Front' came to power in West Bengal in 1977, the Government immediately tried to implement the post independence Land Reform measures. There were a few legal records of rights in case of bargadars who were cultivating the lands of the landowner for a pretty long time. The government also noticed that in spite of having provisions in the

Act to record their right of cultivation as bargadars, few came forward. The rural society was mainly dominated by the land owning group and was managed in such a way that only a few sharecroppers dared to record their names as sharecroppers. So, it was very difficult to protect the interests of the sharecroppers who were not legally recognised as sharecroppers. At this juncture the Government took a drastic measure to bring out the names of the actual sharecroppers by launching a movement called *Operation Barga*.

Operation Barga: Measures

In relation to this 'Operation Barga' movement some amendments were made in 1978 in the previous share Tenancy Acts.

The definition of 'Personal Cultivation' was amended as follows:

I. 'Personal cultivation' means cultivation by the landowner himself either by his own labour or by the labours of any member of his family but not by servants or hired labourers working on wages.
II. The landowner must have a residence either of himself or some members of his family in the locality (within 8 k.m. radius) where the land is situated and must reside at that place during most of the time in a year
III. Income from the land must be his main source of income.

Previously if a bargadar was evicted he could be protected by the Act but now there was provision to punish the landowner for such harassment.

In this amendment it has been laid down that, if a person unlawfully attempts to evict a bargadar he would be punishable. One of the important provisions in the 1978-79 amendments is that any cultivator can claim his record of rights of cultivation as a bargadar, on a particular plot of land of the owner. The responsibility of disproving that claim to that right, vests entirely on the landowner.

The main motive behind operation Barga was:

- To record the rights of cultivation of the bargadars,

- To give the bargadars legal protection against eviction. If a person dies his legal inheritance will also be the legal successor of that barga land.
- To receive a due share by the bargadars and to collect receipt against payment of share from the landowner.

Operation Barga: Strategy

The government noticed the helplessness of the poor bargadars and decide to implement the provisions of Bargadary Acts (1950-1972), in favour of the sharecropper through "*Operation Barga*" movement and amended those Acts as to suit their requirements.

It was decided that the Government officials especially the J.L.R.O, Settlement Officer and the *Kanungo* (a public surveyor) in their areas would find out pockets or areas of intensive barga cultivation. They would consult and take the help of the *Krishak Sabha* in the locality. After locating, the concerned officers in a squad would proceed to the area. They would then organise group meetings of bargadars in the hamlets and prepare a list of bargadars and their counterpart, the land owners of that locality/*mouja* within a short period after issuing public notice. By beat of drum the officers would inform the name of the mouja where an on the spot-inquiry would be undertaken to give record of rights to the actual bargadars. The next day or within a few days, the officers would go to the spot themselves and inquire and examine the plot of land and their actual tillers. In the process of inquiry importance would be given to the testimonials of the actual tillers of the surrounding plots. A *Kancha Parcha* (unconfirmed) would be issued instantly to the actual tillers of the land i.e. bargadars. The *Kacha Parcha* would be replaced after words with a *Pacca*, i.e. confirmed one by the concerned officer.

In the previous Act, provisions were made regarding the share of the produce according to the share of inputs supplied by the bargadars *vis-a-vis* the landowners. The landowner leasing out the land will get 25 per cent of the gross produce as rent. The bargadars who will supply manual labour for cultivation would get 50 per cent of the gross produce. And the rest, i.e. 25 per cent would be divided between the bargadars and the landowner in proportion to the material inputs supplied by them.

In fact the 'Operation Barga' movement was not only an attempt for a legal record of rights to the actual tillers or bargadars but also a movement for enforcement of all the provisions under the previous Acts. This includes the distribution of share of produce between the bargadar and the landowner.

The idea behind this movement was not only to prevent the exploitation of the tenant cultivators by the landowners. It aimed at (i) assuring them of their legal rights on the lands they cultivate, and at the same time (ii) to raise the level of agricultural production and their standard of living and income.

Presently West Bengal is known for its progressive land reform measures. The Left Front Government enacted series of land reform laws in order to modify and improve the land tenure system. These Acts sought to regulate terms and conditions of tenancy, impose ceiling of land holdings, acquire and distribution of land declared surplus under the Land Ceiling Act (vested land) to the landless and marginal farm families. But contrary to the general expectation, even those reforms had hardly brought any better changes as compared to those implemented in some other states of India. Only 77.94 per cent of the acquired land could be distributed to the landless and marginal farmers (the beneficiaries). In the national context the same figure is slightly higher (78.31 per cent). However, the performance of this state is laudable as it has acquired 94.67 per cent and distributed 73.76 per cent of there ported surplus land to 20.44 lakh beneficiaries, which is about 43 per cent of the total beneficiaries in the country, as an average 0.46 acre per beneficiary. The corresponding figures for the country are 87.25 per cent and 68.35 per cent only and the total numbers of beneficiaries are 47.59 lakhs.

It may be observed that efforts in reforms in West Bengal have achieved a significant success in breaking land concentration of the old Zamindari type and providing security to a large body of share-cropping tenants, has created a basis of small-scale peasant economy on a wider scale. The allotment of land had certainly enhanced the social position of the allottees in the rural society. This is evident from the fact that they have now got associated with *village panchayats, gram sabhas* and different political organisations. This also may be partly because of the competition to remain organised in order to discourage the rural vested interest from trying to take back the land. It was noticed that about half of the allottees still have smooth working relationships with their former landlords while the rest could not maintain the earlier relationships. This may, perhaps, be due to the fact that some landlords had lost only very little land and that too of poor quality while some others lost more areas as well as better land.

The socio-economic condition of the allottees have improved, with regard to income, employment, education, housing and social prestige, as a direct result of land distribution. However, the fact remains that the landlords had lost some economic assets, may be marginal in comparison to their overall property is concern, but the landless who did not have any productive assets at all gained substantially. It is natural, therefore, that those all who got less land and poor quality of land, gained less. But it is true that every allottee of surplus land had gained through the programme.

Actually the idea and the methodology of what is now known as Operation Barga evolved during a camp held at Halusai. These camps were aimed at taking the entire official machinery from the district collector downwards to meet the landless and near-landless for a free and frank discussion on their rights, obligations and problems, so as to enable the government to diagnose the root cause of the villager's problems. A squad of functions was formed with officers drawn from the settlement wing and the land management wing under the collectors. The Tribal Welfare Department was associated with the squad in areas where tribal *bargadars* were in large concentration. The purpose of holding meetings with the bargadars was to explain to them the objectives of Operation Barga and to inform them of the benefits that would accrue with recording of their names in the record of rights. The venue of such meetings was stipulated to be as near the places of residence of the bargadars as possible and the genuineness of the government's efforts to protect their rights and interests should be conveyed to them in such meetings. Reconnaissance and field verification was carried out with the objectives of ascertaining the actual state of affairs in the field. This was an extremely important step as the recording of the bargadars was based on it. The information received during the evening meetings regarding barga cultivation were to be verified during the field inquiry and any additional information received was noted for follow up action. When, after such an inquiry, a person was established to be a bargadar, he was to be recorded as such under Section 50 of the Land Reforms Act. The creation of a new class of 33 lakh marginal cultivators, which has been made possible by distribution of vested lands and recording of sharecroppers constitutes a mighty instrument of social transformation. As a result of the Operation Barga, 14,26,264 bargadars were recorded in the state till October 1990.

In recent years, Operation Barga has lost its initial successful focus. Under the guise of official takeover, unscrupulous elements target weak landholders like widows and take over their lands, often leaving them destitute.

The bargadars, moreover, all still vulnerable, particularly economically, as they belong to the lowest strata of rural society and continue to be dependent upon non-institutional sources for credit to meet their cultivation and consumption costs. Hence, only assured and adequate credit from non-traditional sources can accelerate economic growth of the rural areas, free the sharecroppers from the yoke of exploitation, and take Operation Barga to its logical conclusion.

Debates on Operation Barga

In this section, we take stock of the major issues being debated by various scholars as regard to the recent phase of tenancy reforms in West Bengal, particularly in respect of the programme of Operation Barga. It may be recalled that one of the purposes of Operation Barga has been to record all bargadars within a certain period so as to provide security to their tenure and entitle them to the stipulated share of produce as also to credit facilities from institutional agencies for production purpose. In consonance with these objectives, some modifications to the tenancy legislation have also been made. However, the programme of Operation Barga has been subjected to serious criticism by many scholars. While many of the criticisms question the justification of such a programme from an economic point of view, others raise doubt against the whole strategy of agrarian transformation being pursued recently in West Bengal of which Operation Barga is an important part.

The most formidable criticisms against Operation Barga have been voiced by Rudra (1981) and Khasnobis (1981, 1982). On the economic front, Rudra argues that (a) barga recording has not led to any gain in the income of the bargadars; (b) the bargadars who have recorded their names have not been able to use much of modern inputs than before; (c) recording of names by the bargadars has choked the flow of production advances from the landlords to the bargadars; and (d) sharing of cost by the landowners which was gradually emerging as a normal phenomenon in West Bengal has been replaced by non-participation in cost by them. Rudra's other objections were perhaps more interesting. He argues that: (1) barga recording has actually failed to weaken the grip of the rich farmers in as much as nearly 50 per cent of the bargadars have not recorded their names; (2) Operation Barga does not aim at abolition but the perpetuation of tenancy; and (3) the barga system is by no means the foundation of West Bengal's agriculture and the bargadars are by no means the most important section of the toiling masses. In his view, agricultural labourers constitute the most exploited and oppressed section of the rural population but their interest has been sacrificed under the Left Front rule.

Khasnobis praises the genuine political will of the government to promote the interests of the bargadars. But, similar to that of Rudra, he explains how the semi-feudal authority of landlords exercise their control over the tenants to frustrate even a 'reformist' policy such as Operation Barga. In his view, Operation Barga, which tries to record the rights of tenants, approved the intermediary rights of the landowners too. Thus the rent earning authority of non-cultivators, condemned by the bourgeoise democratic revolution, gets a communist sanction. This is the fundamental weakness of the policies adopted by the Left Front Government for the promotion of the interests of the bargadars (Khasnobis, 1981).

There are other criticisms too against Operation Barga. Dutt (1981) is doubtful how long the bargadars can sustain their strength in the absence of economic viability. Bereft of institutional finance and marketing facilities, he argues, the bargadars are bound to the landowner-cum-usurer. He further argues that the Left Front Government seems to have underestimated the degree of penetration of usury and merchant capital in the rural economy. If this were appreciated, more efforts should have been made to consolidate land holdings of poor peasants, to unite them through various forms of cooperatives, which would include labourers but definitely exclude landowners who exploit other's labour. He concludes: 'What seems to be missing still is a sense of direction of the agrarian programme in its broad framework' (Dutt, 1981).

Sengupta (1981) goes on to argue that with near completion of the land reform programmes of the first phase (the so called democratic phase) in West Bengal in terms of abolition of intermidiary interests, acquiring of surplus land for redistribution and barga tenancy reform, the agrarian policies of the Left government have reached their 'saturation point'. He, therefore, asks: 'where does one go from here?'

Defects in the System

It is true that the primary objective of barga recording was to offer tenurial security. With regard to the protection of the rights of the tenants, land reforms programme had much to offer. Intially when the Land Reform Act (LRA) was adopted, a landowner was permitted to evict a sharecropper when the land was nedded for 'personal cultivation'. Eviction of sharecroppers was a common phenomenon in rural Bengal in the fifties and sixties. The Land Reforms Amendment Act of 1971 attempted to stop misuse of provisions relating to 'personal cultivation'. According to the Amendment Act, the land-owner who terminates the cultivation of barga land on the ground of personal cultivation either by himself or by any member of the family will be required under the provision of the Act to live near the land for the most part of the year. Moreover, the main source of earning of the same landowner must be from agriculture. According to the Amendment Act, when a bargadar is evicted from the barga land on the ground of personal cultivation, the same land will have to be cultivated either by the landowner himself or by the members of the family. Under no circumstances the landowners will be allowed to cultivate the same land with the help of wage labourers.

Legislative measures were not enough to improve the living conditions of the sharecroppers. It was necessary to give them tenurial right by some other methods. In order to do so, the government of West Bengal came out with a new method for the registering of the names of sharecroppers. The programme came to be known as 'Operation Barga' (OB). The registration of names was carried out with the help of government workers, panchayat members and peasant organisations. The following steps were taken in this operation. First, identification of priority areas with larger concentration of bargadars; second, formation of official squads for moving into these priority pockets; third, conducting the meeting of the squad with the bargadars and owners preferably in the evening and in a public place; fourth, hearing from both the parties by the government officials and examining documents and finally, passing judgement and issuing the certificates to the bargadars whose names were recorded.

However, attempts were made to enthuse the sharecroppers to use modern agricultural inputs, HYV seeds, irrigation, etc., by offering them loans from banks and cooperatives. It is important to examine these questions at length as for the first time a new experiment was carried out in a State on a massive scale to improve the conditions of sharecroppers. One novel feature of the experiment is that it relied entirely on group action by involving the government officials, elected panchayat members and *Kisan Sabha* activists. Besides, the question of improving productivity under OB, several other issues need close attention, e.g. their social conditions, development of political awareness, etc. Some writers have pointed out that the barga recording has not improved the economic conditions of bargadars. The recorded bargadars have not been using modern inputs and institutional loans have failed to reach the needy sharecroppers. The programme failed to weaken the grip of the rich landowners. Non-recording of names of a large number of sharecroppers also questions its effectiveness. Some writers draw our attention to the fact that instead of abolishing tenurial relations, the West Bengal Government through this programme has legitimised an age-old practice of exploitation through rent.

The present study tried to find out some kinds of transgressing of Barga system, which might cause the premature death of such a novel idea.

Relevance of the Present Study

In West Bengal a series of tenancy reform measures were undertaken since the introduction of Bargadari Act 1950. In the Act the Bargadars (sharecroppers) were recognised as some kind of undertenant. This Act recommended 60 : 40 share in favour of such bargadars who would be responsible for supplying manual labours, draught power, seeds and manures. However, there was no provision for the protection of Bargadar's occupancy rights at the time of West Bengal Estate Acquisition Act, 1954, was promulgated. The primary motive was that to abolish all intermediary rights on land, which the Zamindars were enjoyed from the period of permanent settlement in 1793. In West Bengal Land Reform Act in 1956, provisions were made to protect the sharecroppers from 60 : 40 to 75 : 25 an amendment of the Bargadar Act was made. These Acts, specially, the Bargadari Act, 1972, were no doubt radical for safeguarding the interest of the bargadars.

When the Left Front government came to the power in West Bengal in 1977, the government immediately tried to implement the land reform measures, specially, the tenancy reform measure, i.e. the Bargadari Act of 1972. Envisaging the helplessness of the bargadars, the government decided to implement the provisions of the Bargadari Acts in favour of the sharecroppers through a movement called *Operation Barga*.

As a result, the socio-economic conditions of the allottees have improved with regard to income, employment, education, housing and social prestige, as the direct result of land distribution. However, the fact remains that the landlords had lost some economic assets, may be marginal in comparison to their overall property is concern, but the landless who did not have any productive assets at all, gained substantially.

However, all is not well in the land distribution programme. The allottees have suffered because of the procedural delays, judicial decisions, lack of inputs, capital and technological know-how and overall indifference towards the comparatively weaker sections. Because of these constraints, some peculiar and interesting dimensions of Operation Barga have been cropped up. They are given below:

(a) Numerous cases have been found where crop sharing has not been implemented as per the law and often it goes against the Bargadars' interests.

(b) Mutual arrangements between landlords and the bargadars are widespread and for that reasons neither peasants' organizations nor the Panchayats take appropriate measures to intervene into the cases. There is also random politicking with land reform measures.

(c) Recently, it is observed that sometimes the bargadar compelled to return the barga land to the landowners. It is also found that, landowners sometimes sell the barga to a third party by taking consent from the bargadars, which has no legal basis at all.

The tillers of the land, having usufructuary rights over land, often dispose of their recorded land in favour of the landowners (or to a third party), defeating the very objective of Operation Barga. These reverse processes, along with other reactionary tendencies, are now gaining ground in West Bengal, which remains a model of land reform programme to the country till today.

There is, *prima facie*, a case that the middle class and semi-middle/medium class landholders, who were otherwise employed, used to act as the buffer between the farmer/bargadar and the middlemen/*aratdar* to avoid distress sell of their produce. This class, for various reasons, withdrew themselves from farm operation, placing the bargadar at the mercy of the middlemen, which ultimately force them to compromise their rights. However, it needs to be investigated how far this factor plays a decisive causal role in the emergence of new trends.

3

Thinkers on Land Reforms: A Chronological Intersect

Land reform is a debatable issue. The debate has been inspired by passionate polemics as well as by scientific inquiry. Thus, some argue that land reform is needed to preserve democracy and political stability, while others consider it as a thereat to democracy and free enterprise. Again, from 'reformist' point of view, some say that it is the best way of preserving essential economic and institutional features, while from Marxist point of view, it is needed to bring structural transformation of the society, by smashing the exploitative rural power structure.

The divergence, nevertheless, arise largely from the varying political and ideological points of view taking cognizance of all varieties on view points, our main concern here is to develop an integrated approach to analyze the whole process of agrarian change *vis-à-vis* the essential ingredient of the pattern of reform over a wide span of time.

It is now widely acknowledged that political power structure in poor agrarian economies is largely based upon the land ownership/operational pattern of the rural households. This land ownership/operational pattern releases a set of forces that determines the relationship between the various groups (classes) of farmers. This relationship is better termed as land relation, which in turn is linked to political power relations. If this relationship (say, landlord-tenant) acts as an impediment to the development of productive forces, reform is needed to change this relationship for transforming the structure of the agrarian economies of impoverished developing countries. This indicates that the process of agrarian reform is inherently a political process.

The underlying importance of land reform is to change the exploitative land relations for the development of productive forces. Thus land reform in a nutshell constitutes a strategy of development, which is based on an institutional framework where due to change in land (production) relations, the cultivator can get the fruits of labour. This occurs in such a fashion that cultivators now feel tempted or get incentive to increase their surplus so as to use it for productive purposes as efficiently as possible in speeding up the growth of the economy as a whole **(Mohalanobis, 1963)**. That is to say, we have to develop a "growth strategy" "as opposed to growth-oriented strategy" (i.e. Green Revolution strategy) as a promoter of economic growth built in within the programme of land reform. In this context, land reform is treated as the engine of the surplus generation through which continuous growth of productive forces takes place.

Dharam Narain and Joshi (1969) analyzed the results of the 16th and 17th Rounds of the National Sample Survey in respect to the 8th Round and observed that leased-in area which constituted about a fifth of the operated area in 1953-54, dropped to one-eighth in 1960-61 and to a little more than one-tenth in 1961-62. They raised the questions on the reliability of the figures as indicative of the magnitude of the tenancy and how real was the phenomenon of decline disclosed by the figures. While analyzing the questions, they observed that the evidences suggest a considerable under-reporting of leased-out areas and showed that the figures of leased-in area were, by comparison, far more reliable as indicative of the magnitude of the tenancy.

Bardhan (1970) analyzed the 8th and 17th Rounds of NSS data and observed that rises in the percentage of rural households who act as pure renters so far as land interests were concerned. One explanation of that phenomenon might be that with sub-division of land through inheritance some of the land might get too small for cultivation and with growth of non-agricultural employment opportunities in the rural sector an increasing number of the small land holders might be leasing out all of their land. It was also possible that the large estate of single household had been notionally transferred to a number of households (say, of relatives) and then leased out by the latter back to the single household, giving rise to the phenomenon observed. In the ex-zamindari areas where the absentee landlords have not returned and the tenants have come into direct relationship with the State and the ryotwari areas in continuation of a process that started long before Independence there has been the emergence of the well-to-do sections among the peasant castes who occupy the middle rung in the social structure in much of rural India. Some of these peasant groups have acquired proprietary rights in their land, some were part-owners and part-tenants. But all of them took agriculture much more seriously than when the land was in the hand of intermediaries or than those who still lease out their land. In general, one might say that in the last twenty years a major change has been seen that agricultural land has passed more and more in the hands of those who took more interests in agriculture. Bardhan opined that sooner or later the system would explode; the cracks might not be strictly on capitalist-proletarian lines, but it would be an explosion all the same.

Distribution of land ownership and the forces shaping it over time are usually issues of major policy concern. Acute scarcity of land, a large subsistence sector, and other economic factors leading to an excessive value being put on land ownership per se, create anxieties that an unregulated land market may lead to increasing concentration of land in the hands of large owners. This would not only go against professed egalitarian objectives but might also raise other problems attendant to large-scale tenancy where the owners themselves shun cultivation. In spite of such concern with countering concentration of land-ownership, little attention has been given to the processes and factors that give rise to such concentration.

Rao (1972) observed that the picture of land transfers was far less dramatic and seemed far more understandable in rational terms than was commonly supposed. Thus the picture contained no hint that in the decades preceding the land reforms – the decades with little State-intervention in the area of ownership, leasing land alienation of land – the peasant-proprietorship in the Ryotwari area was fighting as loosing battle against feudalistic forces or that the status-seeker's demand for land was getting precedence over the cultivator's demand for it.

Sanyal (1972) tried to examine the trends in agricultural tenancy between the period 1953-54 and 1961-62 and observed that there might have been an underreporting of tenancy. The possibility of households reporting tenanted area as owned also could not be ruled out.

Chakravarty and Rudra (1973) reviewed that very little empirical study seems to have been made in this country of the economic differences between owner operated farms and tenant operated farms. The general idea was that tenancy is an institution not only detrimental to welfare but also inimical to growth. Because of the lack of security, lack of sufficient returns to investment and absence of incentives to investment, tenant farms were supposed to be run less efficiently than owner operated ones. Theory also goes to support commonsenses, in this respect. Marshallian analysis goes to show how and why, with the same production function, a tenant farmer would give less input and obtain less output than owner cultivators. Of course, the result does not apply to fixed rent tenancy but only to the share-cropping system; and some latter-day theoretical works show (e.g. those of Cheung), even the share-cropping system can be operated with such arrangements as to make inapplicable some of the assumptions of the Marshallian analysis that are crucial for the result concerning inefficiency. But the results of a systematic analysis of data taken from farm management sources however, suggested that there were not very many marked differences in the input-output patterns of owner operated farms and tenant operated farms and that the latter were not run very differently from the former.

In another study **Dwivedi and Rudra (1973)** reiterated the previous findings through analysing another set of more recent data.

Chandra (1974) designated the problems of sharecropping was a dying institution, at least in Bengal. He remarked that in the years since the fall of the second UF Government in West Bengal in 1970, there were reports of widespread eviction of sharecroppers. The basic reason was "extraneous": the landowners were afraid that sharecroppers might acquire permanent occupancy rights sooner or later. Quite often the sharecropper was merely shifted from one plot of land to another belonging to the same landowner; in other cases a new tenant replaces the old one. Rarely does the landlord himself take to cultivation hiring field labourers under his own supervision. Rack-renting through sharecropper's arrangement has generally been found at least as lucrative as farming with hired labour.

One of the assumptions of land reform legislation is that tenants as a class belong to the exploited and the weaker sections, needing protection from landlords of the dominant class. There seems to be enough evidence in recent years to suggest that the picture is not so simple. While a large number of really weak tenants have lost whatever security they had, the dominant class is extending its operational control on land through leasing in. Even if concentration in ownership declines, concentration in operational holdings need not. In fact, the latter concentration is tending to be larger than the former.

Nadkarni (1976) provided further evidence of this developing contradiction in land reforms from a survey of six villages of Marathwada in Maharashtra conducted on the eve of introduction of regular irrigation. It analysed the impact of leasing behaviour on the concentration in operational holdings and studied the class nature of non-cultivating owners of land. In the light of land transfers in the past, it was feared that this trend might further accelerate in the area after the introduction of full-scale irrigation. What makes this development significant was that this was a part of countrywide phenomenon. Hence, it would be necessary for policy-makers to think afresh about where the trust of land reforms should be, if these reforms are intended to be meaningful. He opined that the choice of the policy-maker, therefore, should be: whether to accept the trend towards capitalist concentration in agriculture with the attendant proletarianisation of the rural masses (while trying to reduce its pains as much as possible through, for example, guaranteed rural employment); or direct the thrust of land reforms in future to organise agricultural production on entirely different lines wherein private ownership and control of land should be abolished, with all members of the village becoming members of the production unit on equal status and earning mainly according to work done rather than according to land owned.

Bagchi (1976) inferred that crop-sharing tenancy, in the Indian context could be understood only in the light of how agrarian relations have evolved in the past, and how contradictions between relations of production and forces of production are evolving today in India.

Bardhan (1976) analysed the 1970-71 data and observed that sharecropping seems to be still the predominant form of tenancy in India, except in the South Indian states, and even in the latter states (with the solitary exception of Kerala) more than 40 per cent of tenanted land was under sharecropping. Of course, the form of sharecropping itself is changing, with increasing prevalence of cost-sharing by the landowner particularly in the purchase of new inputs. This has been associated with a rise in the rental share for the landowner in some areas, but not in others. With increased cost-sharing the landlord may be gradually taking a larger role in the entrepreneurial decisions for the small sharecropper's farm and may soon convert the sharecropping system into nothing but a form of owner cultivation with a piece wage system of paying for labour. The dividing line between a crop-sharing tenant and an attached labourer paid a share of the crop has been rather thin all along in any case.

Laxminarayan and Tyagi's (1977) analysis clearly indicates the importance of large holders among tenants, and the unquestionable emergence of crop-sharing tenancy as the dominant form of tenancy in predominantly foodgrain-producing areas. Irrespective of the type of tenancy, all tenancies come in the way of efficient allocation of the resources. Even cost-sharing tenancy arrangements do not lead to optimum utilisation of resources.

Ray (1978) opines that the hypothesis made about the changing structure of lease market in India boils down to two propositions. The first is that for various reasons, ownership of leasable land is increasingly getting distributed among an ever larger number of petty lessors. The second is that simultaneously there has also been a tendency for the leased-in land to get concentrated in fewer hands. In other words, a process of lessors getting smaller and lessees getting bigger is said to have set in.

Chattopadhyay, M. (1979) examined the relative efficiency of the two modes of cultivation – owner cultivation and tenant cultivation – in terms of input-output relationships. The output per bigha was significantly higher in the owner cultivating farms. The inputs too were higher in the owner cultivating farms. However, net income of owner cultivating farms seems to be significantly higher than that of the tenant cultivating farms excluding the cost of family labour input employed in both these types of holdings. He infers that owner cultivators cultivate their lands more intensely – more of labour and non-labour material inputs, better irrigation facilities, multiplicity of remunerative crops etc. Viewed from this angle, owner cultivation seems to be more efficient than tenant cultivation.

Chattopadhyay, S. (1979) observed that it was during the regime of the second United Front (UF) government that an extraordinary jubilation among the peasantry was seen. At that time the movement for unearthing excess lands held by the landlords-jotedars over the ceiling raised high hopes amongst the peasantry. He felt that Operation Barga is not an exception. Rather it has to be made clear that there are many impediments to a rapid recording of sharecroppers. Through successive amendments the West Bengal Land Reforms Act has become really beneficial to the bargadars. All sorts of safeguards for the bargadars have been provided in this Act. Recording of bargadars eliminates all possibilities of their being evicted from the lands, which they cultivate. But in spite of this recording in the last settlement operation was very poor. There is no correct estimate of the total number of bargadars in the state. It may be somewhere in the range 2.2 to 3.5 million. But only 0.4 million had been recorded before the initiation of the Operation Barga. There are mainly three reasons for this poor state of affairs: (1) lack of awareness among the bargadars about their rights, (2) fear of reprisal by the landowners, and (3) economic dependence on the landowners. Again, very few bargadars know that recording of their names gives them protection against eviction. It was also true that the huge task involved in the Operation Barga leaves ample scope for genuine mistakes. The incidence of such mistakes may have been quite considerable. But the Operation barga proceedings are followed by four other stages of work, viz. *Khanapuri-Bhujharat*, attestation, draft publication and final publication of the records. If there is a genuine mistake or a violation of regulations in the Operation Barga proceedings, it can be pointed out or challenged by the interested person at any subsequent stage of the work. The Left Front government has attached utmost importance and urgency to the recording of bargadars for two reasons: (1) once a bargadar is recorded as a bargadar and given a certificate it becomes more difficult for the landowner to evict him than an unrecorded bargadar; (2) the barga-certificate issued to him entitles him to financial assistance from institutional sources, protection against eviction is of vital importance to a bargadar but it has very limited scope for promoting his economic interest. With a view to promoting the economic interest of the bargadars and assignees of vested lands, the West Bengal government has already started a new progarmme. A pilot scheme for providing agricultural credit to some recorded sharecroppers and assignees of vested lands was initiated with the help of public sector banks and co-operative banks. The result of the experiment was by and large encouraging.

Roy Choudhury (1980) reviewed the promises and fulfilment of land reforms in West Bengal. He reviewed the main features of the programme of land reform as: (a) Quick recording of the names of sharecroppers (bargadars) through Operation Barga, thereby securing to them their legal rights; (b) Distributing the already available ceiling surplus vested lands among the landless and land-poor rural workers, in active cooperation with the panchayati raj institutions; (c) Detecting and vesting more ceiling surplus lands, through quasi-judicial investigative machinery with the help of rural workers' organisations and panchayati raj institutions; (d) Giving cover of institutional credit to sharecroppers and assignees of vested land in order to irreversibly snap the bondage they have with the landlords and moneylenders; (e) Assigning permanent title, as permissive possessors, to all landless agricultural workers for homestead purposes (including sharecroppers, artisans and fishermen) who are occupying others' lands of upto 0.08 acres; (f) Providing small sources of irrigation to assignees of vested lands – through bamboo tubewells where underground hydrological conditions permit such technology, and back-financed dugwells with heavy subsidy from the State in other suitable areas – so as to induce such assignees to go in for big-value multiple cropping; (g) Giving financial assistance, in the form of subsidies, to the assignees of vested land for development of their land; (h) Abrogation of the old revenue system, which was a hangover from the zamindari area, and its substitution with a new measure under which revenue is assessed on land-holding above a certain valuation on a progressive rate. Moreover, exemption of small and marginal farmers from revenue; (i) Restoration of alienated land which has been lost by poor and marginal farmers through distress sale, provided the purchaser himself was not a poor peasant with land-holding less than one acre; (j) Designing a Food for Work Programme, in order to develop a rural infrastructure which would benefit primarily the assignees of vested land and marginal farmers and give them sustenance in periods of distress so as to prevent transfer of land to affluent farmers. Of these 10 points in the land reform measures of West Bengal, two are new, viz., the giving of institutional credit, to loosen the hold of the moneylender and landlord, and the abrogation of the old revenue system of the zamindari era. The other measures have been attempted by earlier regimes as well. Choudhury observed the achievements of Operation Barga has not been upto expectations – perhaps because the main task was actually carried out by the administration, with little or no help from the peasants' organisations. Again, curiously enough in the 10-point programmes of land reforms in West Bengal, the Left Front State government has not included any step to ensure statutory minimum wages for agricultural workers. It was also a fact that regarding distribution of vested agricultural land the process was tardy and unsatisfactory in almost all districts. The main reason behind this was the role of vested legal professionals.

According to the West Bengal Land Reforms Act (1955), a *bargadar* is ***a person who under the system generally known as adhi, barga or bhag cultivates the land of another person on the condition of delivering a share of the produce of such land to that person.*** A cultivator under the *kisani* system is also a bargadar in the legal sense of the term. As an economic category, the bargadar is a tenant, often a sharecropping tenant, paying a ground rent to the owner of the soil. The bargadar has no occupancy right over the soil he tills. Usually, he has no written contract with the landowner; the contracts are mostly oral in character, which have no legal validity **(Khasnabis, 1981)**.

Bandopadhyaya (1981) questioned whether the Operation Barga is a success or not? He observed that at an initial stage, OB was marked with spectacular success. Whereas the number of recorded bargadars before beginning of the OB was only about 0.2 million, after the introduction of the OB, the average rate of recording increased by 300 per cent per month. The highest monthly figure was attained in January 1979 when the special OB camps recorded 32,000 bargadars. As a result, between September 1978 and July 1979, 7,32,955 bargadars could be identified and recorded. But the overall success was not satisfactory. Out of the estimated 2 million bargadars, the Land Record Department could register the names of about one million bargadars only. Thus about 50 per cent of the bargadars still remain unregistered. Why were about half of the estimated bargadars unable or unwilling to participate in Operation Barga? The results of a field survey might suggest the answer. There were two empirically stated reasons for such a poor participation in OB. Some of the tenants stated that they had fear of eviction if they tried to record their rights. Faith in mutual relations was the reason submitted by some tenants. A sizable section of the tenants refused to answer this apparently innocent question. It was understood that these tenants, mostly landless and marginal farmers, refused to discuss the question out of an apprehension, that this conversation might be communicated to their landlords, thus producing adverse consequences for themselves. He inferred that, the execution of such a programme requires a fundamental rearrangement of property relations that is unattainable under the present social set-up. The question of a political revolution that does not compromise with the present set-up becomes important.

Operation Barga is nothing but a massive drive to register the names of the sharecroppers with the collaboration of the groups of beneficiaries and with the active assistance of the peasant organisations. Enriched by the experiences of the beneficiaries, the LF government had divided the process of Operation Barga into five stages. These five stages, according to a government circular dated July 5, 1978, were as follows:

(i) **To identify the *mauzas*** (revenue villages) on a priority basis where the sharecroppers are largely concentrated. The basic work is to be done with the help of local peasant organisations.

(ii) **To form squads** consisting of the kanoongo, junior land records officer and amins in order to conduct the whole work. More experienced persons are to be selected for this purpose. Usually the Additional District Magistrate (Land Reform) leads these squads.

(iii) **To organise evening meetings with the beneficiaries**. In these meetings government officials and workers of the different local peasant organisations explain the various advantages of recording of names. Through discussions sharecroppers are made to overcome their fear. These meetings are usually held near the residence of the sharecroppers.

(iv) **Observation and physical verification of the number of bargadars**. Investigating officers should keep systematic notes on it. This work is very essential for the actual recording purpose.

(v) **The recording of the names of the sharecroppers.** In most cases bargadars are given interim certificates of records, after due verification, at the end of 'operation'. **(Ghosh, 1981).**

Dutt (1981) viewed that though the agrarian policies of the Left Front government in West Bengal have enabled the poorer sections of the rural population to become more conscious of their rights, what is missing is a broader sense of direction. It is still not clear if these policies are intended to bring about a small peasant proprietor economy, or whether these aim at a mixed economy where the agricultural labourers and poor artisans will have communal ownership of land, with the government extending support to small producers' cooperatives. Such lack of clarity of aims is perhaps due to the fact that the leading partner of the Left Front government has underestimated the degree of penetration of usuary and merchant capital in rural economy and overestimated feudal exploitation; this probably also explains the importance attached in the Left Front government's agrarian programme to registration of tenancy and land distribution.

If a political party aims at majority support among the agricultural population, it cannot but in the ultimate analysis betray the most exploited and the most oppressed sections of the rural masses. **Rudra (1981)** tried to substantiate this contention in terms of precisely those agrarian programmes of the West Bengal government, which are being publicised as the most significant achievements of the ruling Front, namely, Operation Barga, Panchayati Raj, and the Food for Work Programme. The author also briefly reviews other programmes which have not been taken up by the LF government and over which the government has maintained total silence. These programmes are: enforcement of ceiling laws and confiscation of land above the ceilings for distribution among landless peasants, imposition of tax on agricultural income, and enforcement of minimum wages for agricultural workers. He concludes the paper with these words: as long as there is private property with unequal distribution, social power would gravitate to the handful of those who possess the bulk of social wealth. Any proposition to the contrary is in conformity with liberal theory and not with Marxism. As a matter of fact, supporters of the Left Front seem to be suffering from an optical illusion. Situations are being judged by them not in terms of classes but in terms of party affiliations. Sweeping victory of people declaring affiliation to the Left parties is being interpreted as a sweeping victory of the exploited classes. Tenants belonging to one party are being evicted to give place to tenants belonging to another party. Landless labourers belonging to different parties are fighting with each other for getting little shares of the all too little land available for distribution among them. These are the kinds of struggle that are taking place in the West Bengal villages. These ought not to be mistaken for class struggles.

Against the criticism of reverse tenancy, that is, the tenancy holdings of the large farmers, (this kind of tenancy stands oppose to the commonsense understanding of the tenancy relationship, where one presumes that the tenant is poor and small while the landowner is rich and big). **Dasgupta (1984)** analysed the NSS data (26th Round) and showed that while the proportion of households with 'partly leased-in land' declines with farm size, about one-third of the households in the 5-10 acres category partly lease-in, and about one-fifth those in the 20-25 acres category also report having leased-in a part of the land. This indicates the spread of this practice of 'reverse tenancy', but to put these figures in the proper perspective one should also note that the amount of such leased-in area as a proportion of the total operated land area sharply declines between 5 acres of holding; it is no more than about 8 per cent for the 5-10 acres category, and about one per cent or so for the large size categories. In other words, while the practice is spreading among the richer households, this affects a relatively small proportion of the total cultivated area.

Mishra (1988) while reviewing the land reforms in Bihar found that the success of the land distribution efforts has been insignificant in relation to the number of landless people, most of them have either received unproductive land, or just paper title of the land or else have not been able to bring it under cultivation due to various reasons. He concluded that strong political will is prerequisite for success of any radical measures of land distribution.

Mathur (1988) opined that all is not well in the land distribution programme. His survey work clearly demonstrated that the allottees had suffered because of the procedural delays, judicial decisions, lack of inputs, capital and technical know-how and the overall indifference towards the comparatively weaker sections.

Lieten (1990) exalted with the land reform measures in West Bengal and commented upon the issue he opined that if West Bengal has a better record in the area of land reforms, a large part of the credit must go to the Left Front government. Its initiatives have been directed at achieving maximum results within the framework of the Indian State. A more radical deconstruction of property relations would have been synonymous with self-defeating brinkmanship.

Allen (1995) reviewed the existing theories regarding sharecropping contracts and found that they are not satisfactory when it comes to explaining what is typically observed. Thus, a theory of tenancy contracts based on the endogenous prevention of defaults was developed. In contrast to previous theories, this is capable of explaining the widespread use of share contracts with a 50 : 50 split and is consistent with the coexistence of wage, share and fixed rent contracts, the demise of sharecropping in more developed economies and the fact that share tenancy is often but not always associated with lower productivity than fixed rental land.

Tenancy Reform offers a more promising explanation of the reform-growth link than land redistribution. Compared with the three percent or so of cropped area that was a redistributed under the Left Front land reforms, the proportion of land under share tenancy in West Bengal at the time of Operation Barga was around 7 per cent. A recent study by the **Banerjee and Ghatak (1995)** examines the effects of tenancy reform on productivity. Banerjee and Ghatak's theoretical model is based on the idea that while a higher crop share and greater security might improve the incentives for a tenant to work harder and to supply greater amounts of non-marketable inputs, the removal of the threat of eviction can have the opposite effect. Banerjee and Ghatak found that after controlling for factors such as rainfall, public irrigation and district-specific fixed assets, the growth in the production of *aman, aus* and *boro* rice was positively correlated with the progress of tenancy reform.

Raju (1997) while reviewing the land reforms in India inferred that the steps taken by the government have not made any noteworthy impact on the agrarian structure to reduce, let alone eliminate the inequality in the distribution of land or income or to afford the poor to get access to the land. During the last three decades, the land reforms seriously jeopardize the interest of the landholders. The structural impediments to production and equitable distribution of rural resources are very much in existence.

Murty (1998) has resolved that state intervention in the land lease market becomes a compelling necessecity when the agararian system is beset with certain 'defects'. These may appear in three forms. First, there may prevail disassociation from land-ownership of the vast mass of peasants who are the actual tillers of land. Tenants may constitute too large a proportion among cultivators to disregard their problems. They enjoy, if at all, limited security of tenure and this is at the root of all the tribulations that tenants may have to endure. Second, there may be no incentive for tenants to undertake investment up to a socially desirable level on their leased plots. And, to the extent that investment is suboptima, it may have the effect of impeding the productive efficiency of tenants. Third, contractual terms of tenancy may be exploitative and exploitation may encompass many inter-linked markets of the rural economy.

It was revealed from the **William**'s **(1999)** study that tenancy and land ownership were both targeted by the CPM at the beginning of the Left Front regime as areas in need of direct action to protect the interests of the poorest. In spite of the academic debate surrounding Operation Barga and the government's land redistribution record, these programmes were of little current interest to the villages in 1993. The impact of the land redistribution on the villages was limited due to the small size of land holdings in general. Panchayat Pradhans stated that their was little scope for further redestribution of land. Tenancy reform had brought some material benefits: around half of the tenants had a greater share of the crop than they did 15 years ago, the only one in three tenants received the full government share of 75 per cent. The most dramatic change in relationships over land had come when the CPM gained power locally several *Mahindars* ('attached' agricultural labourers) used this to their own advantage, illegally registering themselves as sharecroppers during Operation Barga. By getting themselves registered with the support of the local CPM, the Mahindars achieved a major political coup: they became tenants with a heriditary right to rent, enabling them to exercise a degree of control over the land previously unheard of. Unsurprisingly, this had caused a great degree of ill-feeling at the time, but 10 years later most general caste farmers were largely resigned to the loss of control of land, and had sought out service employment instead.

4

Study Area and the Context

For the purpose of the study three districts of West Bengal have been selected purposively. The district **Birbhum** has been selected, as it is an agriculturally backward district of West Bengal, where usually one crop can be harvested in a year and has very low cropping intensity. But at present, after having some irrigation mechanisms (like shallow tube-well, submersible pumps etc.), a large number of farmers are harvesting more than two crops in a crop year. Eventually with this development some kinds of contract bargadari system has been developed in the area, which brings a new dimension to the power structure of rural Bengal.

The district **Burdwan** (Bardhaman) has been selected as the district is agriculturally most progressive in the State and designated as the granary of West Bengal. Farmers of the district usually collect more than two crops in a year; naturally the cropping intensity is high. Another important feature is that the farmers of the district are politically more conscious regarding their rights and they were the pioneers of the land reform movement in the State.

The district **Jalpaiguri** is situated in the North of Bengal and its socio-economic characteristics are somewhat different from the former two districts. But mutual arrangements in *bargadari* system have also been reported from the district [Mukherjee and Bandopadhyay, *New Horizons for West Bengal Panchayats*, Report submitted to the Government of West Bengal, 1994].

One block from each district has been selected for the study on the basis of the highest concentration of recorded bargadars in the block. The entire study has been carried out in these three districts taking sample farmers from the villages. The villages from each block have been selected on the basis of highest and lowest concentration of recorded bargadars. Accordingly two villages have been chosen, which have highest concentration and two villages, which have lowest concentration of bargadars as per records.

The sample design can be depicted in the following pictorial form:

STATE		*WEST BENGAL*	
DISTRICTS	*BIRBHUM*	*BURDWAN*	*JALPAIGURI*
BLOCKS	Dubrajpur	Memari – II	Falakata
Gram Panchayats	Jashpur	Kuchut	Dhanirampur-I
Villages	Ghoratari Puchiara Bodakuri Beletore	Nawhati Kasipur Kapastikuri Baje Rasulpur	Jogi Jhora Barabak Narasingpur Mechhna Dhura and Bala Bathan Deomali

Birbhum Sampling

List of Blocks and corresponding number of Bargadars in the District Birbhum

Name of the Blocks	*Total Number of Recorded Bargadars*	*Area in Acres*
Bolpur	8266	9885.24
Dubrajpur	**14,651**	**6524.71**
Illambazar	7804	7203.56
Khoyrasole	13,145	13280.97
Labpur	7912	6401.58
Mayureshwar – I	3114	3198.04
Mayureshwar – II	2632	2252.31
Mhammad bazaar	3854	5197.63
Murarai – I	1927	1782.30
Murarai – II	2653	2959.35
Nalhati	6015	4447.97
Nanoor	9087	6650.53
Rajnagar	5424	13086.35
Rampurhat – I	4191	1520.56
Rampurhat – II	2299	2470.40
Sainthia	7800	9881.56
Suri – I	4344	9578.64
Suri – II	3226	4321.22
Total	**1,10,287**	**1,12,032.31**

It is explicit from the above table that the Block Dubrajpur has the highest concentration of recorded bargadars. Therefore, the **Block Dubrajpur** has been selected for the study.

Out of the nine Gram Panchayats (GP) in the Block, the highest concentration of recorded bargadars has been found in the Jashpur GP.

List of Villages Alongwith Number of Recorded Bargadars in Jashpur Gram Panchayat

Name of the Villages	*Jurisdiction List No.*	*No. of Recorded Bargadars*
Dakshingopalpur	150	30
Aulia	151	30
Rengna	163	76
Birori	164	36
Budhgram	165	14
Khajmahammudpur	166	06
Lohagram	167	55
Puchiara	168	174
Bodakuri	171	14
Krishnanagar	172	49
Jashpur	173	84
Kantari	174	35
Koratari	175	04
Beletor	176	10
Chottosalunchi	199	97
Ghoratari	201	191
Dhagram	202	61
Sajina	220	20
Boro salunchhi	221	64

It is evident from the above table that the villages Ghoratari and Puchiara have the highest concentration of the recorded bargadars and the villages Koratari and Khajmahammudpur have the lowest concentrations. Primarily these four villages have been selected for the purpose of the study. But due to political unrest the author could not enter into the village Khajmahammudpur and Koratari. Thus, in lieu of Khajmahammudpur and Koratari, villages Beletor and Bodakuri have been taken for the study, as they are also the least concentrated villages in respect to the recorded bargadars.

After selection of the villages, a detailed list of recorded bargadars has been collected from the Land Revenue Inspector's Office. Out of the 191 and 174 recorded bargadars in the villages Ghoratari and Puchiara, 50 bargadar households have been taken randomly considering two socio-economic characters, viz. Caste and Land-holdings. Out of the least concentrated villages of Bodakuri and Beletor (number of recorded bargadars are 14 and 10 respectively), 12 and 8 households have been selected randomly following the same selection criteria. Thus, all total of 120 households have taken from these four villages as the primary unit of the study.

Burdwan Sampling

List of Blocks and Corresponding number of Bargadars in the District Burdwan

Name of the Blocks	*Total Number of Recorded Bargadars*
1. Burdwan Sadar-I	2146
2. Burdwan Sadar-II	3908
3. Raina – I	4861
4. Raina – II	5720
5. Ausgram – I	3843
6. Ausgram – II	5720
7. Memari – I	4974
8. Memari – II	11115
9. Jamalpur	3125
10. Khandaghosh	7519
11. Galsi – I	4853
12. Galsi – II	3086
13. Bhatar	6977
14. Barabani	684
15. Salanpur	287
16. Jamuria	4340
17. Raniganj	1126
18. Katwa – I	4081
19. Katwa – II	3392
20. Ketugram – I	4941
21. Ketugram – II	1893
22. Mongalkot	5136
23. Kalna – I	4343
24. Kalna – II	5480
25. Purbasthali – I	1389
26. Purbasthali – II	2589
27. Monteswar	4063

(*Contd.*)

(*Contd.*)

Name of the Blocks	*Total Number of Recorded Bargadars*
28. Kanksa	5848
29. Faridpur – Durgapur	2248
30. Andal	433
31. Pandabeswar	515
Total	**1,21,488**

It is explicit from the above table that out of 31 Blocks in the district, Block Memari-II has the highest concentration of recorded bargadars. Therefore, the Block Memari-II has been selected for the study.

Out of 9 Gram Panchayats (GPs) in the Block the highest concentration of recorded bargadars has been found in the Kuchut GP. Thus, Kuchut GP has been fixed for the study.

List of Villages Alongwith Number of Recorded Bargadars in Kuchut Gram Panchayat in Burdwan District

Name of the Villages	*Jurisdiction List No.*	*No. of Recorded Bargadars*
1. Kaleswar	20	73
2. Basatpur	32	23
3. Kuchut	33	68
4. Masagari	34	67
5. Paikra	35	17
6. Baje Rasulpur	59	08
7. Baragram	60	46
8. Nawhati	61	126
9. Paschim Srerampur	62	17
10. Akalia	63	16
11. Chandipur	64	38
12. Kapastikuri	65	14
13. Rokanpur	117	18
14. Gandhapur	119	37
15. Kanpur	120	43
16. Ganti	121	25
17. Parhati	122	21
18. Madhupur	123	20
19. Tajpur	124	25
20. Kasipur	125	77
TOTAL		**779**

It is evident from the above table that out of 20 odd villages, village Nawhati and village Kasipur have the highest concentration of the recorded bargadars and the villages Kapastikuri and Baje Rasulpur have the lowest concentrations. Primarily these four villages have been selected for the purpose of the study.

After selection of the villages, a detailed list of recorded bargadars has been collected from the Land Revenue Inspector's Office. Out of the 126 and 77 recorded bargadars in the villages Nawhati and Kasipur, 50 bargadar households have been taken randomly considering two socio-economic characters viz. Caste and Land-holdings. Out of the least concentrated villages of Kapastikuri and Baje Rasulpur (number of recorded bargadars are 14 and 8 respectively), complete enumeration has been carried out in these two villages.

Jalpaiguri Sampling

List of Blocks with Number of Recorded Bargadars in Jalpaiguri District (with Different Acts)

Name of the Blocks	*W.B.E.A Act 1953*	*W.B.L.R. Act 1955*	*Operation Barga 1977*	*Total*
1. Jalpaigudi	729	1999	2305	5033
2. Maynagudi	283	1884	1281	3448
3. Malbazar	406	2376	803	3585
4. Dhupgudi	453	2267	2240	5260
5. Raiganj	474	2455	1060	3989
6. Alipurduar-I	1796	2410	973	5179
7. Falakata	2928	3437	2075	8440
8. Alipurduar-II	2201	2929	755	5885
9. Kalchini	758	852	222	1832
10. Kumargram	988	956	2540	4484
11. Nagrakata	500	266	563	1329
12. Madarihat	963	1102	675	2740
Total	**12479**	**22,933**	**15,492**	**51,204**

It is edident from the table that out of 12 blocks, **Falakata** block has the highest number of recorded bargadars in the district. So, Falakata block has been selected for the study at Jalpaiguri district.

List of Gram Panchayats (GPs) in Falakata Block with Number of Recorded Bargadars

Name of the GP	*No. of Bargadars*	*Area (in Acres)*
1. Dhanirampur – I	1026	1191.07
2. Dhanirampur – II	986	1089.13
3. Jatswar – I	657	711.34
4. Jatswar – II	759	853.44
5. Gubarnagar	1015	1144.75
6. Degaon	976	1119.76
7. Salkumar	1005	1183.15
8. Mairadanga	932	1178.76
9. Falakata – I	453	541.62
10. Falakata – II	631	713.32
Total	**8440**	**9626.34**

It is explicit from the table that out of 10 Gram Panchayats, **Dhanirampur–I** Gram Panchayat has the highest number of recorded Bargadars. Therefore, Dhanirampur–I GP has been selected for the study.

ANOMALY IN DATA SOURCE

We had collected data from the ***Falakata*** *block office regarding the highest concentration of recorded bargadars, it had been found that the GP* ***Dhanirampur-I*** *had the highest concentration. But after selecting the GP, when primary survey had been started village wise, we could found surprisingly only 4 villages were there and the number of recorded bargadars were less in comparison to the mentioned recorded data at the block office. However, we did complete enumeration (census) of the village bargadars in those 4 villages.*

Village-wise Number of Recorded Bargadars in Dhanirampur–I GP

Name of the Village	*J.L. No.*	*No. of Bargadars*
1. Jogi Jhora Barabak	01	105
2. Narasingpur	02	44
3. Mechhuodhura Balabathan	03	83
4. Deomali	04	122
Total		**354**

The Context of the Study

It is by now widely acknowledged that political power structure in poor agrarian economics is largely based on the land ownership/operational pattern of the rural households. This land ownership/operational pattern releases a set of forces that determines the relationship between various classes of farmers. This relationship is better termed as land relation, which in turn is linked to political power relations. If this relationship (say, landlord-tenant) acts as an impediment to the development of productive forces, reform is needed to change this relationship for transforming the structure of the agrarian economies of impoverished developing countries.

The underlying importance of land reform is to change the exploitative land relations for the development of productive forces. Thus land reform, in a nutshell, constitutes a strategy of development, which is based on an institutional framework where due to change in land relations, the cultivator can get the fruits of labour. This occurs in such a fashion that cultivators feel tempted or get incentive to increase their surplus so as to use it for productive purposes as efficiently as possible in speeding up the growth of the economy as a whole. In this context, land reform is treated as the engine of surplus generation through which continuous growth of productive forces takes place.

The above arguments thus, suggest that agricultural/rural development may broadly be based on two approaches. One is technological and the other is institutional or structural. Land reform, no doubt, constitutes the institutional or structural approach. It is to be noted here that change in land relations consequent upon the adoption of land reform measures does not bring automatic development of productive forces. For that development, relentless efforts of adopting technological and institutional factors are to be emphasized for transformation of the society at a higher plane.

The primary motivation of land reform is to reduce poverty by reducing inequality. This, however, cannot be achieved without an effective distributive measures. The redistributive land reform is advocated, because smaller farms exhibit higher employment and output. Thus redistributed land reform measures are often justified on the ground of efficiency, equity and justice. As a matter of fact, suggested tenancy reform in isolation (i.e. without redistributive measures) can not go for any desired change, so long as the high incidence of tenancy and the exploitative nature of land market emanate from highly unequal land ownership structure.

We are quite aware that in a land scarce economy, enough land will not be available. What is more important is not the amount of land, but number of peasants who would be the owners of land and would unleash their creative energy to put an end to the stranglehold of the anti-productive vested interest.

Furthermore, empirical evidences suggest that drastic land reform followed by cooperatisation and colletivisation as a long run measures, may facilitate economics of scale, the large-scale introduction of modern technology, increased production and larger agricultural surplus. For the short run, in absence of such cooperatisation and/or collectivisation, any land redistribution programme may even promote small holding agriculture successfully by providing credit and modern inputs effectively.

Land reform basically means breaking up of large land holdings and redistribution of land to landless and small owners. This is also an essential precondition for increasing productivity of land and labour in agriculture. In the Indian context, land reform initially meant for abolition of Zamindari and reform of tenurial system.

Redistribution of land is widely looked upon both a goal as well as means to achieve greater equity, self-respect and self-confidence towards meeting livelihood needs for the families of the rural poor, at the same time serving the wider interests of increased food security and agricultural productivity for the nation as a whole.

The **Primary objectives** of the land reforms programme were to reduce the inequities prevalent in the system of landholding and to increase productivity. The First Five Year Plan enunciated the purpose of the policies as, firstly, to remove such motivational and other impediments to increase in agricultural production as arise from the agrarian structure inherited from the past, and, secondly, to eliminate of exploitation and social injustice within the agrarian system so as to ensure equality of status and opportunity to all sections of the rural population.

The **secondary objectives** were linked to the specific measures.

1. Abolition of intermediaries;
2. Tenancy reforms;
3. Ceiling on agricultural holdings;
4. Prevention of fragmentation of holdings;
5. Land consolidation.

In West Bengal, the Bargadari Act of 1950 recommended a 60 : 40 share in favour of such sharecroppers who were supplying the means of production and seeds and manure. But it did not provide for the protection of sharecroppers from possible eviction. Further, there was no provision for compulsory recording of sharecropping rights. Given these shortcomings effective implementation was out of the question. In fact, the Bargadari Act, 1950 did herald the period of growing legislative attention to the problem of bargadars, so numerous yet unrecognised, its immediate practical effect was to provoke a large-scale eviction of bargadars by landowners from their traditional possessions. All records admit of eviction of bargadars on an unprecedented scale in the 1959s and early 1960s.

Maximum use was made of the loopholes in the law by legal and extra-legal means. Thousands of acres were illegally retained; fictitious charitable trusts and endowments were created. Arable lands were converted into lakes, fisheries and orchards. In the face of the tremendous offensive launched by the vested interests in land through such means, the affected peasantry was helpless. Further amendments were made subsequently. In 1971 amendment had been adopted for augmenting the share of the sharecroppers form 60 : 40 to 75 : 25. In 1975, amendments were made for homestead land acquisition. Finally came the West Bengal Landholding Revenue Act, 1979 and the Revenue Rules of 1980. The three most outstanding features in this respect provided for in the 1979 amendments were the following:

1. The responsibility of disproving a claim to bargadari rights was squarely put on the landowners.
2. Personal cultivation was defined as cultivation on the basis of physical participation by members of the landowners' family.

3. A stringent residential clause, stipulating residence of the claimant to resumption within a distance of five miles from the plot of land claimed, was introduced.

These three features together decisively tilted the judicial provisions in favour of the practicing bargadars.

The Left Front Government came to power with an effective majority in 1977. In view of its experiences during two earlier shorter terms (1967 and 1969), the Front took seriously about the implementation of the land reform measures already enacted during the last two decades. What is novel about Operation Barga is that the drive to register the names of sharecroppers (to ensure their legal rights) is undertaken with the active assistance of not only the bargadars themselves but also of rural workers' organisations and self-governing institutions. Operation Barga, launched by the end of 1978, directed land reform officials to conduct group meetings with the potential beneficiaries. Tentative lists of bargadars were prepared after such meetings and published for verification on the next day. After the field verification a provisional list was hung up in all important places in the villages. Landowners were given the opportunity to file objections. Thereafter, certificates of sharecropping were distributed among the beneficiaries.

In order to protect the interests of the bagradars the following restrictions were imposed by the Act, in a situation where the landowner will be entitled to terminate cultivation by a bargadar:

- If a bargadar fails to cultivate the Land or uses it for other than purposes of cultivation,
- If a bargadar does not cultivate the land personally,
- If the bargadar fails to tender the due share of the produce to the land owner, and
- If the landowner require the land for bringing it under personal cultivation.

But there is a provision that a landowner cannot simply evict a bargadar on the plea of bringing the land under personal cultivation. The restrictions imposed are as follows:

1. A land owner cannot evict his bargadar for his personal cultivation if his total land under personal cultivation exceeds three hectares.

2. The landowner is not entitled to evict a sharecropper if by such termination the total land cultivated by a bargadar is reduced to less than one hectare. However, a bargadar under this Act may be evicted if he cultivates, an excess of six hectares.

The Bargadar Act, 1972 was no doubt radical for safeguarding the interests of the bargadars. But due to lack of effective implementation of the measures, on the one hand and vigorous offensive measures undertaken by the landowner against the bargadars on the other, the provisions of the Act were of little use to the bargadars. The bargadars also had no easy access to the *Bhagchas* office or civil court.

The main motive behind Operation Barga was:

- To record the rights of cultivation of the bargadars,
- To give the bargadars legal protection against eviction. If a person dies his legal inheritance will also be the legal successor of that barga land,
- To receive a due share by the bargadars and to collect receipt against payment of share from the landowner.

In a nutshell, the idea behind this movement was not only to prevent the exploitation of the tenant cultivators by the landowners. It aimed at (i) assuring them of their legal rights on the lands they cultivate and at the same time (ii) to raise the level of agricultural production and their standard of living and income.

The socio-economic condition of the allottees have improved, with regard to income, employment, education, housing and social prestige, as direct result of land distribution. However, the fact remains that the landlords had lost some economic assets, may be marginal in comparison to their overall property is concern, but the landless who did not have any productive assets at all gained substantially. It is natural, therefore, that those all who got less land and poor quality of land gained less. But it is true that every allottee of surplus land had gained through the programme.

The most formidable criticisms against operation barga had been voiced by Rudra (1981). On the economic front, Rudra argued that (a) barga recording has not led to any gain in the income of the bargadars; (b) the bargadars who have recorded their names have not been able to use much of modern inputs than before; (c) recording of names by the bargadars has choked the flow of production advances from the landlords to do the bargadars; and (d) sharing of cost by the landowners which was gradually emerging as a normal phenomenon in West Bengal has been replaced by non-participation in cost by them. In his view, agricultural labourers constituted the most exploited and oppressed section of the rural population but their interest had been sacrificed under the Left Front rule.

There are other criticisms too against Operation Barga. Dutt (1979) was doubtful how long the bargadars could sustain their strength in the absence of economic viability. Bereft of institutional finance and marketing facilities, the bargadars were bound to be under the clutches of landowner-cum-usurers. If this were appreciated, more efforts should have been made to consolidate land holdings of poor peasants, to unite them through various forms of cooperatives, which would include labourers but definitely exclude landowners who exploit other's labour.

However, attempts were made to enthuse the sharecroppers to use modern agricultural inputs, HYV seeds, irrigation, etc., by offering them loans from banks and cooperatives. It is important to examine these questions at length as for the first time a new experiment was carried out in a sate on a massive scale to improve the conditions of sharecroppers. Besides, the question of improving productivity under Operation Barga, several other issues needs close attention, e.g. their social conditions, development of political awareness, etc.

It is evident from the study that the barga recording has not improved the economic conditions of bargadars. The recorded bargadars have not been using modern inputs and institutional loans have failed to reach to the needy sharecroppers. Non-recording of names of a large number of sharecroppers also questions its effectiveness.

The allottees have suffered because of the procedural delays, judicial decisions, lack of inputs, capital and technological know-how and overall indifference towards the comparatively weaker sections. Numerous cases have been found where crop sharing has not implemented as per the law and often it goes against the Bargadars' interests. Mutual arrangements between the landlords and the bargadars and between the landlords and the vested land groups are widespread and for that reason neither peasants' organization nor the Panchayat could take appropriate measures by intervening into the cases. There is also random politicking with the land reform measures. Recently, it is observed that sometimes the bargadar compelled to return the barga land to the landowners. It is also found that, landowners sometimes sell the barga land to a third party by taking illegal consent from the bargadars.

On the contrary, a growing dissent is being cropped up in the landowners' part. They felt that they are deceived by the bargadars because by taking the advantage of power politics and 'command law' the bargadars are continuously depriving them on various aspects. Neither the bargadars bother to give the stipulated share to them, nor they ready to hear the landowners' suggestion about the cultivation and cropping pattern. So it is not true that all the landowners are villain as made by the sympathetic theoreticians of the land reforms, they are victim too of the system.

The tillers of the land, having usufructuary rights over land often dispose of their recorded land in favour of the landowners (or to a third party), defeating the very objective of operation barga. These reverse processes, along with other reactionary tendencies, are now gaining ground in West Bengal, which remains a model of land reform programme to the country till today. Throughout the entire journey of the work, the author tried to identify the number of transgressing efforts adopted in different districts having various agro-climatic and development perspectives and found out the causes and consequences of such transgressions.

5

Beneficiaries of Land Reforms

In this chapter the beneficiaries of land reforms have been accounted in regard to their agricultural land holdings in the study area. The term sharecropper denotes here to identify the unrecorded bargadars in contrast to the bargadars, who have recorded their lands under Barga regulations.

Table 1A depicts the villagewise distribution of the households (H.H.) of the study area in Birbhum District according to their social status related to the agricultural lands.

Table 1A: Agricultural Landwise Stratification of Birbhum Households

Villagers	*Owner Farmer*	*Share Cropper*	*Bargadar*	*Pattadar*	*Landless*	*Total H.H.*
Pachhiara	196	–	174	90	78	538
Ghoratari	203	–	191	117	121	632
Bodakuri	41	–	14	36	37	128
Beleturi	37	–	10	41	37	125
Total	**477**	–	**389**	**284**	**273**	**1423**

In the four studied villages of Birbhum, there were total 1423 households. Among the head of these households 477 were owner farmers, 389 were bargadars, 241 were Patta holders and 273 were Landless people who were engaged in different occupations like shop keeping, hair cutting, agricultural labour, daily wage labour, blacksmith, mason and transport agents. Villagewise distribution of the categories of house holds has been documented clearly in Table 1A.

Table 1B explicits the villagewise distribution of the households of the study area in Burdwan District according to their social status related to agricultural lands.

In the four villages of Burdwan district there were total 982 households. Among the head of these households 302 were owner farmers, 140 were sharecroppers, 225 were Bargadars, 146 were Pattaholders and 169 were Landless who were engaged in different occupations like agricultural labour, daily wage labour, shopkeeper, different other whole sale businesses, hair cutting, black smithing and transport agents. Only 22 bargadars have got the possession of small amount of Patta land along with their Barga land (who were purposively excluded from the list of patta holders). Village wise distribution of these households can be observed from the Table 1B.

Table 1B: Agricultural Landwise Stratification of Burdwan Households

Villagers	*Owner farmer*	*Share Cropper*	*Bargadar*	*Pattadar*	*Landless*	*Total H.H.*
Kasipur	91	43	77	56	59	326
Naohati	129	72	126	64	75	466
Kabastikuri	56	23	14	20	29	142
Baje Rasulpur	26	2	8	6	6	48
Total	**202**	**140**	**225**	**146**	**169**	**982**

- 22 Bargadars have not been counted in Patta holder list though they have got some amount of Patta land.

Out of the four villages of Jalpaiguri district there were total 2403 households. Among the head of these households, 513 were owner farmers, 201 were sharecroppers, 405 were bargadars, 860 were Patta holders and 424 were Landless who were engaged in different occupations like agricultural labour, tea garden labour, daily wage labour, shopkeeper, different whole sale businesses, hair cutting, black smith and transport worker. Village wise distribution of these categories of households can be observed from Table 1C.

Table 1C: Agricultural Landwise Stratification of Jalpaiguri Households

Village	*Owner farmer*	*Share Cropper*	*Bargadar*	*Pattadar*	*Landless*	*Total H.H.*
Jogi Jhora Barabak	217	86	108	142	146	699
Narisngpur	72	26	83	268	89	538
Mechhna Dhura Bala Bathan	35	21	92	226	56	430
Deomali	189	68	122	224	133	736
Total	**513**	**201**	**405**	**860**	**424**	**2403**

Beneficiaries of Land Reforms

The present study confines among the land reform beneficiaries and they are categorized into three groups: (i) Bargadars (ii) Agricultural Land Patta Holders and (iii) Homestead Land Patta Holders.

Bargadars

Table 2A depicts the ethnic group wise and Barga Land categorywise distribution of Birbhum Bargadars.

Table 2A: Ethnic Group and Land categorywise Distribution of Birbhum Bargadars

Barga Land Holding Category (in Acre)	*GC*	*SC*	*ST*	*M*	*Total Bargadar*	*Total Land (in Acre)*
Below 1	38	88	–	119	245	214.13
1– < 2	9	28	1	38	76	124.47
2– < 3	4	15	2	12	33	93.57
3– < 4	1	–	–	16	17	62.785
4– < 5	–	4	1	9	14	59.94
5– < 6	–	2	–	1	3	5.43
6– < 7	–	–	–	1	1	6.78
Total	**52**	**137**	**4**	**196**	**389**	**567.105**

It could be traced out that among the Bargadars of Birbhum district, majority were Muslims (M) and then came up Scheduled Caste (SC) category. If we look from the view point of land possession, majority of the bargadars belong to below one acre of land holding category and they were also holding the major portion of total barga land. The Scheduled Tribes (ST) are negligible in number as recorded bargadars even less than the General Castes (GC).

Table 2B: Ethnic Group and Land Categorywise Distribution of Burdwan Bargadars.

Barga Land Holding Category (in Acre)	*GC*	*SC*	*ST*	*M*	*Total Bargadar*	*Total Land (in Acre)*
Below 1	9	32	16	101	158	68.02
1– < 2	4	5	7	27	43	54.61
2– < 3	2	4	2	8	16	36.66
3– < 4	1	–	1	2	4	14.47
4– < 5	–	–	–	2	2	8.52
5– < 6	–	–	–	2	2	10.60
Total	**16**	**41**	**26**	**142**	**225**	**192.88**

Table 2B demonstrates the ethnic group and Barga land holding wise distribution of Burdwan district Bargadars.

Like Birbhum district, among the total bargadars of Burdwan district, Muslims were very much dominating in number. Again, most of the bargadars were belong to below one acre of land category and they were holding the majority of total barga land. Here altogether 225 Bargadars were holding 192.88 acres of Barga land.

Table 2C: Ethnic Group and Land holdingwise Distribution of Jalpaiguri Bargadars

Barga land Holding Category (in Acre)	*Ethnic Groups*				*Total Bargadar*	*Total Land (in Acre)*
	GC	*SC*	*ST*	*M*		
Below 1	16	18	54	24	112	54.88
1– < 2	19	28	43	11	101	143.42
2– < 3	18	13	31	15	77	188.65
3– < 4	12	10	18	9	49	173.64
4– < 5	5	11	9	4	29	124.12
5– < 6	2	3	5	4	14	75.04
6– < 7	1	2	7	1	11	71.94
7– < 8	–	–	1	2	3	22.08
8– < 9	–	–	1	–	1	8.83
9– < 9.91	–	–	1	4	5	47.31
9.91 & above	1	–	2	–	3	38.36
Total	**74**	**85**	**172**	**74**	**405**	**948.27**

Unlike Birbhum and Burdwan districts, it has been observed that majority of the bargadars were Scheduled Tribes in Jalpaigudi district and then comes the Scheduled Castes. Again, majority of the bargadars belong to below one acre of land category but they did not hold major lands. Maximum number of land was in the hands of 3 to less than 4 acres of land holding category (Table 2C).

The Agricultural Land (Agri-Land) Patta Holders

Table 3A depicts the ethnic group wise Agri-land patta holders of Birbhum district.

Table 3A: Ethnic Group and Land Categorywise distribution of Birbhum Agri-Land Patta holders

Patta Agri-Land Holding Category (in Acre)	*GC*	*SC*	*ST*	*M*	*Total Patta Holder*	*Total Land (in Acre)*
0.01 – 0.05	–	–	–	–	–	–
0.06 – 0.10	–	5	–	2	7	0.56
0.11 – 0.15	1	4	–	10	15	1.875
0.16 – 0.20	2	7	–	5	14	2.76
0.21 – 0.25	–	8	–	17	25	5.86
0.26 – 0.32	1	18	–	20	39	11.28
0.33 – 0.40	3	77	13	29	122	45.17
0.41 – 0.45	–	9	–	8	17	7.35
0.46 – 0.50	3	5	–	5	13	6.13
0.51 – 1.00	2	13	1	9	25	18.67
1.01 & above	–	1	–	6	7	7.285
Total	**12**	**147**	**14**	**111**	**284**	**106.84**

Among the patta holders, majority belongs to 0.33-0.40 acre of land category and also they were holding the maximum land out of the total land. Again majority of the patta holders belong to Scheduled Caste group. Total 284 patta holders were holding 106.84 acres of agricultural lands.

Table 3B demonstrates the ethnic group and land category wise distribution of Burdwan Agri-land patta holders.

Table 3B: Ethnic Group and Land Categorywise distribution of Burdwan Agri-Land Patta holder

Patta Agri–Land Holding Category (in Acre)	*GC*	*SC*	*ST*	*M*	*Total Patta Holder*	*Total Land (in Acre)*
0.01 – 0.05	2	–	–	7	9	0.36
0.06 – 0.10	1	16	13	19	49	3.81
0.11 – 0.15	–	12	6	18	36	4.68
0.16 – 0.20	1	9	5	19	34	6.12
0.21 – 0.25	–	8	5	9	22	5.14
0.26 – 0.32	–	2	2	2	6	1.75
0.33 – 0.40	–	4	1	2	7	2.63
0.41 – 0.45	1	–	1	1	3	1.30
0.46 – 0.50	–	–	–	2	2	0.98
Total	**5**	**51**	**33**	**79**	**168**	**26.77**

Here, majority of the patta holders were Muslims. Again majority of the patta holders were belong to 0.06-0.10 acre of patta land holding category and majority of the lands were in the hands of 0.16-0.20 acre of land holding category. Total 168 patta holders were holding 26.77 acres of agricultural land in the study area.

Table 3C: Ethnic Group and Land Categorywise distribution of Jalpaiguri Agri-Land Patta holders

Patta Agri-Land Holding Category (in Acre)	*Ethnic Groups*				*Total Patta Holder*	*Total Land (in Acre)*
	GC	*SC*	*ST*	*M*		
0.01 – 0.05	4	28	19	14	65	2.17
0.06 – 0.10	9	23	–	11	43	3.12
0.11 – 0.15	12	12	34	–	58	6.62
0.16 – 0.20	26	31	–	14	71	12.26
0.21 – 0.25	15	16	31	14	76	16.44
0.26 – 0.32	4	21	23	–	48	14.54
0.33 – 0.40	6	88	20	12	126	44.82
0.41 – 0.45	12	–	28	1	41	17.55
0.46 – 0.50	–	4	45	15	64	30.72
0.51 – 1.00	59	62	129	17	267	200.10
1.01 & above	–	1	–	–	1	1.63
Total	**147**	**286**	**329**	**98**	**860**	**349.97**

In Jalpaiguri district, majority of the Patta holders were Scheduled Tribes. The maximum number of Patta holders were belong to 0.51 – 1 acre of land holding category and they also holding the major amount of patta lands (Table 3C).

The Homestead Land Patta Holders

In the study areas of Birbhum, only 11 homestead land patta holders were holding 0.15 acre of homeland. The total 10 Scheduled Caste patta holders were holding 0.01 acre of land each and only one Muslim patta holder was holding 0.05 acre of land.

Table 4B depicts the ethnic group wise distribution of Burdwan homestead land patta holders.

Here, majority of the patta holders were belong to below 0.01 acre of homestead patta land holding category and majority of homestead patta lands were in the hands of more than 0.02-0.03 land holding category patta holders. Again majority of the homestead patta holders were Scheduled Tribes in this case.

Table 4 B: Ethnic Groupwise Homestead Patta Land holding categories of Burdwan District.

Homestead Patta Land Holding Category (in Acre)	*GC*	*SC*	*ST*	*M*	*Total Patta Holder*	*Total Land (in Acre)*
Below 0.01	–	12	29	2	43	0.42
> 0.01 – 0.02	–	8	23	2	23	0.39
> 0.02 – 0.03	–1	9	27	1	38	1.105
> 0.03 – 0.04	3	5	13	5	26	1.01
> 0.04 – 0.05	1	3	8	4	16	0.79
> 0.05 – 0.06	–	2	14	1	17	1.00
> 0.06 – 0.07	–	–	2	5	7	0.47
> 0.07 – 0.08	–	–	1	3	4	0.30
Total	**5**	**39**	**117**	**23**	**184**	**5.455**

Table 4 C: Ethnic Groupwise Homestead Patta Land holding categories of Jalpaiguri District

Homestead Patta Land Holding Category (in Acre)	*Ethnic Groups*				*Total Patta Holder*	*Total Land (in Acre)*
	GC	*SC*	*ST*	*M*		
Below 0.01	–	5	1	–	6	0.05
> 0.01 – 0.02	–	6	1	–	7	0.101
> 0.02 – 0.03	12	–	17	–	29	0.637
> 0.03 – 0.04	19	28	69	25	141	5.076
> 0.04 – 0.05	–	46	19	40	105	4.988
> 0.05 – 0.06	6	20	33	14	73	4.103
> 0.06 – 0.07	3	8	21	5	37	2.483
> 0.07 – 0.08	44	59	137	16	256	19.998
Total	**84**	**172**	**298**	**100**	**654**	**37.436**

(Out of total 654 patta holders, 546 have got Agri-patta also)

It is noticeable that in Jalpaiguri district, 654 homestead patta holders were holding 37.436 of homestead patta lands. Among them majority were belong to more than 0.07 – 0.08 homestead land holding category. Surprisingly, they all were bargadars and with barga recording they have acquired these patta lands for homestead. Among the total patta holders most dominating caste was Scheduled Tribes (Table 4C).

6

Bargadars and the Transgressors

West Bengal Land Reforms Act, 1955 under Section 2(2) defines Bargadar as: *"Bargadar" is a person who under the system generally known as adhi, barga or bhag, cultivates the land of another person on condition of delivering a share of the produce of such land to that person; and includes a person who under the system generally known as kisani, cultivates the land of another person on condition of receiving a share of produce of such land from that person.*

After complete enumeration of the study areas in three districts, we have divided the Bargadars into two different categories on the basis of their operation. The first category is designated as the **General Bargadars**, who recorded their names and maintaining the rules and regulations of Barga and the second category has been designated as the **Transgressors** who were somehow deviating from the existing rules and regulations of present Barga system. The distribution of these two types of Bargadars in the three districts are as follows:

Table 5: General and Transgressor Bargadars in the Study Area

Districts	*Total No. of Bargadars*	*No. of General Bargadars*	*No. of Transgressors*
Birbhum	389 (100)	282 (72.49)	107 (27.51)
Burdwan	255 (100)	159 (70.67)	66 (29.33)
Jalpaiguri	405 (100)	222 (54.81)	183 (45.19)

Note: Parentheses indicate the percentage to total.

From Table 5 it is clear that the number of transgressor bargadars in Jalpaiguri district is higher than the other two districts. That implies the cases of anomalies in regard to Barga system are more pronounced in North Bengal in West Bengal.

Though the study has been conducted to identity the transgressor bargadars and to find out the deep rooted causal factors responsible for that, before going to discuss in details about them, it is imperative to know the socio-economic characteristics of the General Bargadars so that a detailed picture of the Barga system could be envisaged.

In this analysis, the land categories have been classified according to the Bargadar's total operational holding. In the study areas of Birbhum district, no bargadar has his own land except Barga land, so his operational holding implied his barga land exclusively. But in Burdwan district, majority of the Bargadars have their own land and hence their operational holding has been calculated by summing up these two types of land they possess. For our convenience, we have categorized the operational holdings into these following groups with specific nomenclatures.

(i) Those, who have below 1 acre of operational land, are termed as *Marginal Farmers*.
(ii) Those, who have 1 to less than 2 acres of operational land, are termed as *Small Farmers.*
(iii) Those, who have 2 to less than 3 acres of operational land, are termed as *Semi Medium Farmers.*
(iv) Those, who have 3 to less than 4 acres of operational land, are termed as *Medium Farmers.*
(v) Those, who have 4 and above 4 acres of operational land, are termed as *Large Farmers.*

Profile of the General Bargadars

In this section the conditions of General Bargadars, who have recorded their lands and sticking to the existing rules and regulations of barga system properly and satisfactorily will be discussed thoroughly.

It is observed from Table 6A, in Birbhum district, a sum of 282 General Bargadars have been accounted in the study area. Among them majority (63.83%) are marginal farmers and mostly belong to the Muslim community (51.42%). Out of the total operational holding amounted to 402.61 acres possessed by all the categories of Bargadars, marginal farmers are holding the maximum (39.07%) of land. The average land holding of the Bargadar is counted to 1.43 acres.

Table 6A: Ethnic Group and Operational holdingwise distribution of Birbhum General Bargadar

Operational Land Holding Category (in Acre)	*Birbhum General Bargadar*					
	GC	*SC*	*ST*	*M*	*Total Bargadar*	*Total Land (in Acre)*
Marginal	25	68	–	87	180 (63.83)	157.32 (39.07)
Small	7	19	–	32	58 (20.57	94.99 (23.59
Semi–medium	3	8	1	7	19 (6.74)	53.87 (13.38
Medium	1	–	–	11	12 (4.25)	44.32 (11.01)
Large	–	4	1	8	13 (4.61)	52.11 (12.95)
Total	**36 (12.76)**	**99 (35.11)**	**2 (0.71)**	**145 (51.42)**	**282 (100)**	**402.61 (100)**

Table 6B: Ethnic Group and Operational holdingwise Distribution of Burdwan General Bargadars

Operational Land Holding Category (in Acre)	*Burdwan General Bargadar*					
	GC	*SC*	*ST*	*M*	*Total Bargadar*	*Total Land (in Acre)*
Marginal	3	10	9	51	73 (45.91)	31.52 (13.21)
Small	2	5	6	23	36 (22.64)	47.88 (20.07)
Semi–Medium	4	2	2	18	26 (16.35)	64.77 (27.15)
Medium	1	7	–	10	18 (11.32)	66.92 (28.05)
Large	–	–	–	6	6 (3.78)	27.48 (11.52)
Total	**10 (6.29)**	**24 (15.09)**	**17 (10.69)**	**108 (67.93)**	**159 (100)**	**238.57 (100)**

From Table 6B it is clear that in Burdwan district a total of 159 General Bargadars have been found in the study area and they possess 238.57 acres of land. Among them majority (45.91%) are marginal farmers and also majority of them belong to the Muslim community (67.93%). But unlike Birbhum bargadars, here maximum land is in the hands of semi-medium and medium farmers. The average land holding of the Burdwan General bargadars has been calculated as 1.50 acres.

In both the districts, Muslims have a general tendency to lease out lands within their own community. For this, Muslim Bargadars are the majority in number and also holding the maximum lands in both the districts.

Table 6C: Ethnic Group and Operational Holdingwise distribution of General Bargadars, Jalpaiguri

Operational land holding category (in Acre)	*Jalpaiguri General Bargadar*				*Total Bargadar*	*Total Land (in Acre)*
	Ethnic Groups					
	GC	*SC*	*ST*	*M*		
Marginal	7	9	11	13	40 (18.02)	31.12 (5.78)
Small	17	15	27	11	70 (31.53)	108.39 (20.12)
Semi-Medium	16	7	21	14	56 (25.22)	136.36 (25.31)
Medium	9	3	10	9	31 (13.96)	105.96 (19.67)
Large	6	5	5	9	25 (11.26)	156.85 (29.11)
Total	53 (23.87)	39 (17.56)	74 (33.33)	56 (25.22)	222 (100)	538.68 (100)

From Table 6C, it is evident that in Jalpaiguri district, 222 General Bargadars possess 538.68 acres of operational land. Among them majority are small farmers but maximum barga land has been possessed by the large farmers. The average land holding of the bargadars is 2.43 acres. Majority of these Bargadars are Scheduled Tribes.

Family Size

Table 7: Ethnic Groupwise distribution of the Family size in the districts

Ethnic Group	*Birbhum*	*Burdwan*	*Jalpaiguri*
GC	6.08 (219)	6.70 (67)	6.62 (351)
SC	5.16 (511)	5.00 (120)	5.21 (203)
ST	6.00 (12)	5.06 (86)	6.18 (457)
M	8.19 (1188)	7.07 (764)	8.02 (449)

Note: Parentheses indicate the total population.

In the studied districts average family size of the Muslims is the highest followed by the General Castes (Table 7).

Table 8: Ethnic Groupwise Literacy Status of the Bargadar Households

(per family, except 0-6 years of age)

Ethnic Groups	*Birbhum*		*Burdwan*		*Jalpaiguri*	
	Illiterate	*Literate*	*Illiterate*	*Literate*	*Illiterate*	*Literate*
GC	2.42	2.67	1.89	3.33	4.15	1.60
SC	2.48	1.84	1.53	2.84	3.15	1.10
ST	1.00	–	2.12	2.18	4.64	0.69
M	4.62	1.31	1.67	4.22	6.09	1.05

In Birbhum among the General Caste families almost 50 per cent are literate whereas in other ethnic groups above 70 per cent family members are illiterate. But in case of Burdwan above 50 per cent family members of all ethnic groups are literate (Table 8). The condition of Jalpaiguri district in this regard is worse than any other districts.

Now we will shift our attention towards their economy and economy related activities.

Occupations

The average family size and dependent population of different land categories of barga households of Birbhum are higher than the corresponding Burdwan bargadar households. Again the number of service holders and businessman population in Burdwan is much higher than the Birbhum and Jalpaiguri where the farmers engaged in agriculture/labour occupation is higher in Birbhum. It has been observed that in Birbhum the subsidiary occupation of the majority of farmers is agriculture/daily labour and very few are engaged in Business and other occupations (rickshaw pullers, mason etc.). But in Burdwan district a number of population is engaged in business and other occupation subsidiarly (Table 9).

Table 9: Population, Economic and Occupational Status of the Barga Households in the Districts.

(Average per household)

District	Operational Land Category (in Acre)	No. of H.H.	Total Population	Average Population	Economic Status		Primary Occupation				Subsidiary Occupation		
					Earner	Dependent	Cultivation	Service	Business	Agri/Daily Labour	Agri/Daily Labour	Business	Others
BIRBHUM	Marginal	180	1211	6.73	2.34	4.39	1	–	–	1.34	0.93	0.02	0.06
	Small	58	403	6.95	2.52	4.43	1	–	0.03	1.49	0.88	0.02	0.10
	Semi-Medium	19	122	6.42	1.89	4.53	1	–	0.05	0.84	0.63	–	–
	Medium	12	99	8.25	1.75	6.50	1	0.08	0.17	0.5	0.17	–	–
	Large	13	92	7.08	1.46	5.62	1	0.08	0.30	0.08	–	0.08	–
BURDWAN	Marginal	73	475	6.51	2.27	4.24	1	0.01	0.11	1.15	0.93	0.03	0.04
	Small	36	229	6.36	2.11	4.25	1	–	0.33	0.78	1	–	–
	Semi-Medium	26	1.64	6.31	2.31	4.00	1	0.08	0.69	0.54	0.42	0.35	–
	Medium	18	113	6.28	1.78	4.50	1	0.17	0.50	0.11	–	0.17	–
	Large	6	38	6.33	1.50	4.83	1	–	0.5	–	–	0.17	–
JALPAIGURI	Marginal	40	251	6.28	1.6	4.68	1	–	–	0.6	1	–	–
	Small	70	463	6.61	1.89	4.72	1	–	0.04	0.85	0.88	–	0.12
	Semi-Medium	56	385	6.87	1.71	5.16	1	0.02	0.09	0.60	0.43	0.04	–
	Medium	31	186	6.00	1.48	4.52	1	0.39	0.06	0.03	–	0.32	0.19
	Large	25	175	7.00	1.40	5.60	1	0.24	0.16	–	–	0.60	–

As Burdwan is agriculturally advanced and crops can be cultivated in three seasons, the economic status of the farmers are better in comparison to other two districts. Again, due to better communication and infrustructural facility the jobs are mostly diversified in the district.

But Birbhum district is agriculturally backward and the major area is totally mono-cropped. So for their bare subsistence the people have to find out other sources of income. As the area is remote and the infrstructural and communication facilities are very poor, so most of them are engaged themselves in agricultural/daily labour occupations and very few can get other jobs.

In Jalpaiguri, it is difficult to find out even suitable subsidiary occupation, what to speak of enough available primary occupations.

Income and Expenditure Pattern

In Birbhum, the marginal, small, semi-medium and medium bargadars are suffering from acute marginal surplus over expenditure. Though the surplus of large bargadars is not worthmentioning, yet they enjoy a better position than other categories of farmers (Table 10).

Table 10: Annual Income and Expenditure of the General Bargadar Households

(*in Average*) (*in Rs*)

District	*Operational Land Category*	*Total Income (I)*	*Total Expenditure (E)*	*Surplus Over Expenditure (I-E)*
BIRBHUM	Marginal	11698.41	11541.08	157.33
	Small	16922.93	14863.47	2059.46
	Semi-Medium	25428.27	23038.10	2390.17
	Medium	29136.18	27921.95	1214.23
	Large	42076.30	33748.56	8327.74
BURDWAN	Marginal	21742.96	20601.37	1141.59
	Small	33197.38	29998.13	3199.25
	Semi-Medium	58649.61	47951.32	10698.29
	Medium	91206.84	70673.50	20533.34
	Large	116021.47	79856.69	36164.78
JALPAIGURI	Marginal	9778.90	9316.70	462.83
	Small	18971.55	17092.60	1878.95
	Semi-Medium	24027.08	21900.11	2126.97
	Medium	29595.94	25821.48	3774.46
	Large	58073.40	42506.75	15566.65

Again it has been noticed that the income of every categories of bargadars of Burdwan is more than the corresponding categories of Birbhum and Jalpaiguri bargadars. The expenditure is also showing the same picture.

Birbhum is basically known as a mono-cropped area and the job diversification is not up to the mark. So the income of the Barga households is very poor. Again due to large family size their expenditure on families is fairly high. As a result the surplus remains negligible and living standard is among the lower rung of the economic ladder.

On the contrary, Burdwan is known as a multi-cropped area with better cropping intensity. Most of the bargadars can cultivate their lands in all three seasons – rainy, winter and summer. So their income from agriculture goes high. Again due to better job availability even in non-farm sectors, a good portion of their household members are engaged in different occupations. As a result their household income remains noteworthy.

In Jalpaiguri the surplus over expenditure of marginal, small and semi-medium categories are very poor. Only large farmers having noteworthy surplus over their expenditures (Table 10).

Agriculture

After examining the social and economic conditions of the General Bargadars, it is imperative to focus on the scenario of their primary occupation i.e. agriculture on which their subsistence depends.

Land Situation

Table 11A: Distribution of Agricultural land of General Bargadars in Birbhum District

(in Acres)

Operational Land Holding Category	*Total Owned Land*	*Total Barga Land*	*Total Land*	*Average Land*
Marginal	–	157.32	57.32	0.87
Small	–	94.99	94.99	1.64
Semi-Medium	–	53.87	53.87	2.84
Medium	–	44.32	44.32	3.69
Large	–	52.11	52.11	4.01
Total	–	402.61	402.61	1.43

In Birbhum no bargadar has his owned land. Their subsistence totally depend on their barga lands. Here the marginal bargadars are holding the majority of land whereas the medium bargadars are holding the lowest amount of land. Total 282 bargadars are cultivating 402.61 acres of land and average land holding per family is 1.43 acres (Table 11A). The average land holding is uneconomic for a technically feasible cultivation proposition.

Table 11B: Distribution of Agricultural land of General Bargadars in Burdwan District

(in Acres)

Operational Land Holding Category	*Total Owned Land*	*Total Barga Land*	*Total Land*	*Average Land*
Marginal	11.91	19.61	31.52	0.43
Small	18.08	29.80	47.88	1.33
Semi-Medium	24.45	40.32	64.77	2.49
Medium	30.25	36.67	66.92	3.72
Large	5.38	22.1	27.48	4.58
Total	90.07 (37.76)	148.5 (62.4)	238.57 (100)	1.50

In Burdwan all land holding categories of the bargadars have their owned land along with barga lands. Here, the major amount of land is in the hands of semi-medium and medium land holding bargadars. Out of total 238.57 acres of land under the Bargadars, 37.76 per cent are owned land and 62.24 per cent are barga land. The average land holding per family is 1.50 acres, which is marginally higher than Birbhum (Table 11B).

Table 11C: Distribution of Agricultural Land of General Bargadars in Jalpaiguri District

(in acres)

Operational Land Holding Category	*Total Owned Land*	*Total Barga Land*	*Total Land*	*Average Land*
Marginal	–	31.12	31.12	0.78
Small	–	108.39	108.39	1.55
Semi-Medium	–	136.36	136.36	2.44
Medium	–	105.96	105.96	3.42
Large	–	156.85	156.85	6.27
Total	–	538.68	538.68	2.43

In Jalpaiguri no bargadar has his owned land. Their subsistence totally depends on their barga land. Here large bargadars are holding the major amount of land whereas the lowest holder is the marginal bargadars. Their average land holding is 2.43 acres which is the highest than the rest two districts (Table 11 C).

Agricultural Support System

Agricultural support system can be found very useful to the farmers who are keen to improvise their agricultural businesses. A weak support system is bound to be embodied with a bleak, negatively inclined agricultural scenario for a particular area or farm situation.

It can be best judged by the machineries and implements, which are supposed to be extensively used for augmenting production.

Machineries and Implements

Table 12A: Agricultural Machineries and Implements of Birbhum Bargadars

Items	*Percentage of Bargadar Households Having Agricultural Implements*				
	Marginal	*Small*	*Semi–medium*	*Medium*	*Large*
Plough	–	–	10.51	33.33	69.23
Bullock Cart	–	–	10.51	33.33	69.23
Submersible/Shallow	–	–	–	–	–
Powertiller/Tractor	–	–	–	–	–
Sprayer	–	–	–	8.33	23.07
Thresher	–	–	–	–	7.69

In Birbhum, the marginal and small bargadars have no owned agricultural machineries and implements. Even very few of other categories have plough, bullock cart, sprayer and threshers. No bargadar has submersible/shallow tube well for irrigation and power tiller/tractor for land tilling. Who have no owned machineries and implements, hire it from the local market, which may cause low production due to non availability at proper time for agricultural operation (Table 12A).

Table 12B: Agricultural Machineries and Implements of Burdwan Bargadars.

Items	*Percentage of Bargadar Households Having Agricultural Implements*				
	Marginal	*Small*	*Semi-medium*	*Medium*	*Large*
Plough	27.40	44.44	46.15	88.88	33.33
Bullock Cart	27.40	44.44	46.15	88.88	83.33
Submersible/Shallow	–	–	–	11.11	33.33
Powertiller/Tractor	–	–	–	–	66.66
Sprayer	–	5.56	15.38	33.33	83.33
Thresher	–	–	3.85	22.22	100.00

In Burdwan, more or less 50 per cent of the marginal to semi-medium bargadars have their owned bullock carts and ploughs and very few of small and semi medium bargadars have their owned sprayers and threshers. None of these categories have their submersible/shallow tubewells and power tiller/tractors. In case of medium bargadars except plough and bullock cart, other owned machineries and implements are very rare. But most of the large bargadars have all types of machineries and implements for their agricultural operations (Table 12B).

Due to poor economic condition and agricultural backwardness of the area, the Birbhum bargadars are unable to purchase sufficient agricultural machineries. But in Burdwan district, due to agricultural advancement, well communication and infrastructural facilities, and due to their better economic conditions, a good number of bargadars have become able to purchase their own machineries and the others who do not possess these implements by their own, they can hire these machineries easily from local market and from their fellow farmers during agricultural operations.

The studied area of Birbhum is a totally mono-cropped area. There is no irrigation facility and the agriculture totally depends on canal irrigation and the vagaries of monsoon. The district has been suffering from acute water shortage and unavailability of irrigation machineries like submersible and shallow tube well aggravates the situation.

Due to absence of powertiller and tractor in the Birbhum study area, all the bargadars use plough (by hiring from local market and from big land owners) for the purpose of ploughing the land. Those who depend on hired plough, their agricultural operation starts in late season due to non-availability of tilling machineries at due time. But in Burdwan area, irrigation facility is much better and the use of tractor/power tiller (also by hiring, which is easily available) is very much frequent, as a result they can start agricultural operation at proper time and also can cultivate the lands at least for two seasons.

Table 12C: Agricultural Machineries and implements of Jalpaigari Bargadars

Items	*Percentage of Bargadar Households Having Agricultural Implements*				
	Marginal	*Small*	*Semi–medium*	*Medium*	*Large*
Plough	–	–	19.64	87.10	100.00
Bullock Cart	–	–	5.36	87.10	100.00
Submerrible/Shallow	–	–	–	–	–
Power tiller/Tractor	–	–	–	–	–
Sprayer	–	–	–	–	48.00
Thresher	–	–	–	–	12.00

In Jalpaiguri, marginal and small bargadars have no owned agricultural machineries and implements even very few of other categories have owned plough, bullock cart, sprayer and thresher (Table 12C).

Cropping Pattern

Table 13: Cropping Pattern

District	*Crops (with variety)*		
	Kharif (Paddy)	*Rabi (Potato & Mustard)*	*Summer (Boro Paddy)*
Birbhum	Swarna Lagu, IR – 36	Potato – Jyoti Mustard – B9	–
Burdwan	Red Swarna	Potato – Jyoti Chandramukhi Mustard – B9	IR – 36 IR – 64
Jalpaiguri	PNR – 381, Anyada – 4094	Potato – Nepali, Punjab, Jyoti, Mustard – B9	Swarna, Chinaboro

Swarna Laghu is the dominating Kharif paddy variety in Birbhum. Some bargadars cultivate IR – 36 also. Boro cultivation is disrupted due to lack of irrigation facilities. Even in Rabi seasons potato (var-Jyoti) and mustard (variety – B9) are cultivated in some patches of lands.

In Burdwan almost all the Bargadars cultivate their lands in three seasons. The Kharif paddy Red Swarna is being cultivated covering the entire acerage. In Boro season, above 70 per cent of lands are covered with Boro paddy (var – IR – 36 or IR – 64) and in small patches of land they cultivate Rabi potato (var – Jyoti or Chandramukhi). Only the medium and large Bargadars cultivate potato in a good amount of land and also they cultivate mustard in tiny land areas for home consumption only.

In Jalpaiguri, almost all cultivators cultivate their land in rainy (Kharif) season only. Very few cultivate their land depending upon tank irrigation in winter and summer season. They cultivate PNR – 381 and Anyada – 4094 HY Paddy in Kharif season. Only few medium and large bargadars cultivate their land in winter and summer season. They cultivate Potato (Nepali, Panjab, Jyoti) and Mustard (B9) in Rabi season and paddy Swarna and Chinaboro in summer season (Table 13).

Share Ratio

In Birbhum district, four types of share of produce have been observed between landowners and bargadars. These are 25 : 75, 50 : 50, 60 : 40 and 15 : 85 in favour of landowner and bargadar. In the district, majority (68.44%) of landowners belong to 25 : 75 share ratio categories. Whereas 21.28 per cent landowners fall under 50 : 50, 7.09 per cent fall under 60 : 40 and only 3.19 per cent landowners fall under 15 : 85 share of produce ratios.

In Burdwan three types of share of produce ratios have been observed between the landowners and Bárgadars. These are 25 : 75, 50 : 50 and 20 : 80 in favour of landowners and bargadars. Majority (54.72%) of the landowners belong to 50 : 50 share ratios whereas 39.62 per cent and only 5.66 per cent fall under 25 : 75 and 20 : 80 share of produce ratios respectively.

Table 14A: Distribution of Birbhum Bargadars According to Share Ratio

Operational Land Holding Category	Share of Produce Ratio (Landowner: Bargadar)			
	25 : 75	50 : 50	60 : 40	15 : 85
Marginal	146	26	6	2
Small	31	19	8	–
Semi–Medium	8	4	1	6
Medium	5	3	3	1
Large	3	8	2	–
Total	193 (68.44)	60 (21.28)	20 (7.09)	9 (3.19)

Note: Parentheses indicate the percentage to total.

Table 14B: Distribution of Burdwan Bargadars According to Share Ratio

Operational Land Holding Category	Share of Produce Ratio (Landowner: Bargadar)		
	25 : 75	50 : 50	20 : 80
Marginal	35	32	6
Small	16	19	1
Semi-Medium	4	22	-
Medium	7	10	1
Large	1	4	1
Total	63 (39.62)	87 (54.72)	9 (5.66)

Note: Parentheses indicate the percentage to total.

In Birbhum as the production is very poor, so the owners have become least interested to augment the production. They think that whatever is coming without any investment is enough for them. For this the majority of landowners belong to 25 : 75 and 15 : 85 share of produce ratios. Where the landlords get 25 per cent and 15 per cent share of the produce respectively without investing anything.

But in Burdwan production is very high and the land gives a lump sum earning in all three seasons a year. So most of the landowners are very much interested to augment the production and also they invest for production even they bear 50 per cent cost of cultivations in the form of inputs except providing labour input. The rest of the two categories of landowners invest nothing.

Table 14C: Distribution of Jalpaiguri Bargadars According to Share Ratio

Operational Land Holding Category (in Acre)	*Share of Produce Ratio (Landowner: Bargadar)*		
	25 : 75	*50 : 50*	*15 : 85*
Marginal	36	4	–
Small	55	12	3
Semi–Medium	38	15	3
Medium	22	8	1
Large	19	5	1
Total	170 (76.58)	44 (19.82)	8 (3.60)

In Jalpaiguri three types of share of produce ratios have been observed between landowners and bargadars. These are 25 : 75, 50 : 50 and 15 : 85. Here majority (76.58%) of the landowners belong to 25 : 75 share ratios. Whereas 19.82 per cent falls under 50 : 50 and only 3.60 per cent landowners fall under 15 : 85 share of produce ratios.

Similar to Birbhum, in Jalpaiguri district, farmers are very poor and no farmer has the knowledge about modern agricultural practices. For this recurring poor production phenomenon and the landowners are not interested in investing on agriculture.

The Transgressors

After the thorough discussion about the socio-economic condition of the General Bargadars, we have accumulated the preliminary knowledge about social, agricultural and economic position of the General Bargadars of the three districts Birbhum, Burdwan and Jalpaiguri of West Bengal.

Now we will shift our attention towards the Anomaly Bargadars of the districts, who or whose landlords are somehow infringing the Bargadari Act under Land Reforms Act – 1955.

It has been observed in Birbhum District that the landowner and bargadar classes are the supporter of opposite political parties. As a result, the negative impact of political interference is much frequent in this area. But in Burdwan, in most of the cases both the landowner and bargadar are the supporters of the same political party. Therefore, in this district, any litigation arises out of political interference, the leading political party always tries to solve it through mutual settlement.

Again it has been observed in both the district that at the time of Operation Barga when the landowners came to know that their share croppers or *mahinders* would register the land under Bargadari Act, they used to offer the bargadars a good amount of money to restrain themselves from Barga recording. Thus some landowners have saved their lands from barga recording and after that they have kept the land under their personal cultivation. Though these types of cases are very much frequent in both the district but the strong political interference have only been observed in Birbhum.

Previously it has been discussed that in Birbhum out of total 389 Bargadars 107 (i.e. 27.51%) and in Burdwan out of total 225 Bargadars 66 (i.e. 29.33%) are transgressors (anomaly bargadars) who are anyhow violating the Bargadari Act of Land Reforms Act, 1955.

Table 15A: Ethnic Group and Land Category wise distribution of Anomaly Bargadars in Birbhum

Operational Land Holding Category	*GC*	*SC*	*ST*	*M*	*Total*	*Total Land (in Acre)*
Marginal	13	20	–	32	65 (60.75)	56.81 (34.53)
Small	2	9	1	6	18 (16.82)	29.48 (17.92)
Semi-Medium	1	7	1	5	14 (13.07)	39.70 (24.13)
Medium	–	–	–	5	5 (4.68)	18.465 (11.23)
Large	–	2	–	3	5 (4.68)	20.04 (12.19)
Total	16 (14.95)	38 (35.51)	2 (1.87)	51 (4.67)	107 (100)	164.495 (100)

Note: Parentheses indicate the percentage to total.

In Birbhum total 107 transgressors are holding 164.495 acres of land that is entirely falls under barga land and they have no owned land. The majority (47.67%) of these Bargadars are belonging to Muslim community fallows by the scheduled caste bargadars (35.51%). Again majority (60.75%) of these bargadars though fall under marginal categories, hold maximum (34.53%)

amount of operational land. The astonishing feature is that with the increase of land category the number of anomaly bargadars are decreasing abruptly (Table 15A). Therefore, anomalies or infringement of Barga Act has been found most in lower land holding cases than medium or large bargadars.

Table 15B: Ethnic Group and Land Categorywise Distribution of Anomaly Bargadars in Burdwan

Operational Land Holding Category	*GC*	*SC*	*ST*	*M*	*Total*	*Total Land (in Acre)*	*Owned (in Acre)*	*Land in (in Acre)*
Marginal	2	8	4	16	30 (4.45)	18.64 (19.34)	7.49	11.15
Small	4	2	2	12	20 (30.30)	28.38 (29.46)	17.11	11.27
Semi-Medium		2	2	1	5 (7.57)	11.84 (12.29)	7.11	4.73
Medium		5	1	4	10 (15.17)	32.96 (34.21)	19.14	13.82
Large				1	1 (1.51)	4.53 (4.70)	1.12	3.41
Total	6 (9.09)	17 (25.76)	9 (13.64)	34 (51.51)	66 (100)	96.35 (100)	51.97 (53.94)	44.38 (46.06)

Note: Parentheses indicate the percentage to total.

In Burdwan district, 66 transgressors (anomaly bargadars) are holding 96.35 acres of land out of which 53.94 per cent are owned land and 46.06 per cent are barga land. Like Birbhum, here also majority (51.51%) of the bargadars are Muslim fallows by Scheduled Castes (25.76%). Again, though majority (45.45%) of the bargadars are marginal in land size category, maximum land (29.46%) is in the hands of small bargadars (Table 15B).

In Jalpaiguri district, a total of 183 transgressor bargadars are holding 409.59 acres of barga land and they have no owned land. Here majority of the Bargadars are belonging to Scheduled Tribe community follows by Scheduled Castes. Again majority of these bargadars are marginal farmers but major portion of barga land held by the big cultivators (Table 15C).

Table 15C: Ethnic Group and land Category wise distribution of Anomaly Bargadars in Jalpaiguri

Operational Land Holding Category (in Acre)	*Ethnic Groups*				*Total*	*Total Land (in Acre)*
	GC	SC	ST	M		
Marginal	9	9	43	11	72	23.76
Small	2	13	16	–	31	35.03
Semi-Medium	4	6	10	1	21	52.29
Medium	3	7	8	–	18	67.68
Large	3	11	21	6	41	230.83
Total	21	46	98	18	183	409.59

Table 16: Types of Transgresses (Anomalies) At a Glance

	Types of Anomalies	*Birbhum*	*Burdwan*	*Jalpaiguri*
1.	Sub-leasing of the Bargaland to the Third Party.	4 (3.74)	1 (1.51)	6 (03.28)
2.	Mortgaging Barga Land	9 (8.41)	2 (3.03)	13 (07.10)
3.	Selling out Barga Land	6 (5.61)	9 (13.64)	27 (14.75)
4.	Political Eviction.	1 (0.93)	N.A	N.A.
5.	Forceful Acquisition of Barga Land by Landowner.	1 (0.93)	N.A	3 (1.64)
6.	Cultivation Barga Land through Mutual Understanding.	1 (0.93)	1 (1.51)	34 (18.58)
7.	Mutual Distribution of Barga Land between all the heirs after the death of Bargadar.	8 (7.48)	3 (4.55)	10 (05.46)
8.	Use of Barga Land in non-agricultural purpose.	N.A	1 (1.51)	N.A.
9.	No share of Produce to Landowner.	26 (24.30)	17 (25.76)	24 (13.12)
10.	Poor Production. (but still not evicted)	51 (47.67)	32 (48.49)	49 (26.78)
11.	Encroachment of Barga land By Industries	N.A.	N.A.	5 (02.73)
12.	Barga recording by the relatives	N.A	N.A.	9 (04.92)
13.	Excessive Holding of Barga lands	N.A.	N.A.	3 (01.64)
Total	Number of Anomaly Bargadars found.	107 (100)	66 (100)	183 (100)

Note: Parentheses indicate the percentage to total.

Transgression: A Case by Case Analysis

Case No. 1: Subleasing the Barga Land to the Third Party

This section of Bargadars was cultivating their lands since long. Because of their poor operational holding, the earnings from agriculture were very meager. So their economic conditions were poor and also deteriorated in such a way that they became unable to continue their agricultural operations. For this they were compelled to sub-lease the lands to some third parties. In this contractual system the share ratio between the third party and the Bargadar remains 3:1 in Kharif (monsoon) and in Boro (summer) seasons. The Bargadars have no investment on cultivation but have some return in this system.

In Birbhum, 75 percent actual landowners of these lands remain in dark about the whole incidence. Interestingly the Bargadar maintained his share ratio with the landowner by suppressing the figure of actual production. Say, the 3rd party has produced 6 quintals of paddy per bigha. According to the share ratio the bargadar is getting 1.5 quintals of paddy per bigha as 25 percent of his share. Now the bargadar gives the information to the landowner that he was produced 4 quintals paddy per bigha and so the landowner is entitled to get 1 quintal of paddy per bigha as his share. Thus the bargadar gets a profit of 0.5 quintal of paddy per bigha without investing any labour and capital from his side. This anomaly has been observed among the marginal and small Scheduled Caste and semi medium Muslim Bargadars. In case of remaining 25 percent cases of Birbhum and all the cases of Burdwan the actual landowners of these lands know the whole incidence and the Bargadars deprive them from any kind of share of produce. This type of anomaly has been observed among the marginal Muslim Bargadars of Birbhum and also of Burdwan.

This section of Bargadars should be convicted under the following sections of West Bengal Land Reforms Act, 1955.

West Bengal Land Reforms (Bargadar) Rules, 1956 has kept a provision under section 17 (I) that the authority appointed by the State Government can terminate the cultivation right of Bargadar if:

(a) The Bargadar has without any reasonable cause failed to cultivate the land or has used it for any purpose other than agriculture.
(b) The land is not cultivated by the Bargadar personally.
(c) The bargadar has failed to tender deposit to the full extent of the share of the produce as required by Sub-section (2) or sub-section (40) as the case may be of section 16 to the landowner.
(d) That the person (having less than 3 hectares of land) owning the land requires it bona fide for bringing it under personal cultivation.

Again Section 15 states in sub-sections that:

1. The provisions of clauses (b) and (c) of sub-section (4) of section 4 shall not apply to the holding of a raiyat or any part of it, which is cultivated by a bargadar so long as cultivation by a bargadar continues.
2. The right of cultivation of land by bargadar shall be heritable and shall not be transferable.

The causes of incidence observed:

In Birbhum 4 bargadars (3.74 per cent) have been traced out who are holding 6.54 acres of barga land have leased out their barga land to third parties. The anomaly has been observed in the marginal, small and semi-medium categories of bargadars (Table 17A).

Table 17A: Distribution of Bargadars under Case No. (1) in Birbhum

Opertaional Land Holding Category (in Acre)	*Ethnic Groups*					*Total Land*
	GC	*SC*	*ST*	*M*	*Total*	
Marginal	–	1	–	1	2	1.84
Small	–	1	–	–	1	1.78
Semi-Medium	–	–	–	1	1	2.92
Medium	–	–	–	–	–	–
Large	–	–	–	–	–	–
Total	–	2	–	2	4	6.54

In Burdwan under this anomaly only one Bargadar has been traced out. He is marginal farmer and Muslim and holding only 0.70 acres of land out of which only 0.16 acre is barga land (Table 17B).

Table 17B: Distribution of Bargadars under Case No. (1) in Burdwan

Operational Land Holding Category (in Acre)	*Ethnic Groups*					*Acre Total Land*	*Owned Land*	*Leased in Land*
	GC	*SC*	*ST*	*M*	*Total*			
Marginal	–	–	–	1	1	0.70	0.54	0.16
Small	–	–	–	–	–	–	–	–
Semi-Medium	–	–	–	–	–	–	–	–
Medium	–	–	–	–	–	–	–	–
Large	–	–	–	–	–	–	–	–
Total	–	–	–	1	1	0.70	0.54	0.16

Table 17C: Distribution of Bargadars under Case No. (1) in Jalpaiguri

Operational land Holding Category (in Acre)	*GC*	*SC*	*ST*	*M*	*Total*	*Total Land (in Acre)*
Marginal	–	–	–	2	2	0.52
Small	–	1	3	–	4	4.68
Semi-Medium	–	–	–	–	–	–
Medium	–	–	–	–	–	–
Large	–	–	–	–	–	–
Total	–	1	3	2	6	5.20

In Jalpaiguri under this anomaly total 6 bargadars have been traced out, who are holding 5.20 acres of land. Here the majority of the Bargadars are small farmers and also holding the major amount of land. Three ethnic communites SC, ST, and Muslim are involved in this kind of anomaly (Table 17C).

It is clear from Table 18 that the Bargadars involved in leasing out their barga lands to the third parties are mostly illiterate and have large family size. Therefore their dependency ratio is high. That can also be evident from Table 19, where it is explicit that besides their Barga cultivation they are mostly engaged in daily labour activities.

Table 18: Demographic features of the Sample Bargadars under Case (1)

District	*Land Category*	*Family Member*	*Literacy Status (except 0-6 years)*	
			Literate	*Illiterate*
Birbhum	Marginal	3.5	1.5	2
	Small	6	–	4
	Semi-medium	12	2	4
Burdwan	Marginal	6	1	5
Jalpaiguri	Marginal	6.50	1.00	5.00
	Small	5.50	0.75	4.25

Table 19: Occupational Status of Sample Bargadars under Case (1)

District	*Land Category*	*Economic Status*		*Primary Occupation*		*Subsidiary Occupation*	
		Earner	*Dependant*	*Cultivator*	*Agri/Daily Labour*	*Agri/Daily Labour*	*Business*
Birbhum	Marginal	1.5	1.5	–	1.5	–	1
	Small	2	4	1	1	1	–
	Semi-medium	2	10	1	1	–	1
Burdwan	Marginal	1	5	1	–	1	–
Jalpaiguri	Marginal	1	5.5	–	1	–	1
	Small	1.75	3.75	–	1.75	–	–

Table 20: Status of Operational Holding of the Sample Bargadars under Case (1)

(Average Per household in Acre)

District	Land Category	In the Past			At Present		
		Owned	Leased in	Total	Owned	Leased in	Total
Birbhum	Marginal	–	0.52	0.52	–	–	–
	Small	–	1.78	1.78	–	0.64	0.64
	Semi-medium	–	2.92	2.92	–	2.25	2.25
Burdwan	Marginal	0.54	0.16	0.70	0.54	–	0.54
Jalpaiguri	Marginal	–	0.26	0.26	–	–	–
	Small	–	1.17	1.17	–	–	–

In Birbhum no bargadar had/has his owned land. At present after subleasing of land the marginal bargadar has no land for cultivation though other categories have very few land for agricultural operation. In Burdwan, only one Bargadar falls under this case. He had his owned land. He had also a very little amount of bargaland, which he had leased out to third party totally. Now he is operating his owned land only. In Jalpaiguri district, the marginal and small Bargadars, fall under this case, was operating with only barga lands. But at present, after subleasing the barga lands, they became landless labourers (Table 20).

It is explixit from Table 21, that before subleasing, their income over expenditure was marginally positive. This amount has been reckoned as their investment for the next cropping year. But the surplus over expenditure was so meager that one cannot think of running better agriculture with that cash in hand. As a result gradually they became unable to maintain their agricultural operations and started subletting their whole or a part of land to the third party (the third party is obviously a owner cultivator of that locality). But their economic situation could not be uplifted with the gesture of subletting their barga lands. Even the situation is worsened. It has been found that after subleasing of barga land, the surplus over expenditure of all categories of Bargadars in all three districts has become negative. So they remain indebted throughout the year (Table 21).

Table 21: Economic Status of the Sample Bargadars under Case (1)

(Average per household in Rs.)

District	Land Category	In the Past (Annual)					At Present (Annual)				
		From Agriculture		Total Income–Expenditure Status			From Agriculture		Total Income–Expenditure Status		
		Income	Expenditure	Income	Expenditure	Surplus	Income	Expenditure	Income	Expenditure	Surplus
Birbhum	Marginal	4012.20	977.80	10620.70	10600.3	20.40	304	-	8612.50	9022.50	-410
	Small	13969.25	3000.25	23374.25	22947.25	427	5807.00	1091.25	15212.40	15238.50	-26.10
	Semi-medium	27915.80	6942.90	34720.80	34618.95	101.85	20233.95	4144.00	25038.00	25134.00	-96.00
Burdwan	Marginal	15165.70	6642.30	22484.00	21987.80	496.40	11571.60	5091.00	18942.00	19566.56	-624.56
Jalpaiguri	Marginal	1346.75	538.66	5461.75	5926.35	-464.60	-	-	5169.30	5337.85	-168.55
	Small	7002.60	2163.80	10852.60	10919.75	-67.15	-	-	7800	8341.50	-541.50

Moreover, the Bargadars fall under this category, have no agricultural support system except spade, khurpi and sickle. The other improved instruments and machineries are very expensive and that too are not available at the time of need. All these Bargadars took loans for purchasing bullock cart and bullocks under IRDP scheme and crop loans from PACS. But it is very much painful that they have no bullock and cart at present, and they have not repaid the IRDP and crop loan amount still now. The abject poverty along with landlessness and debt trap acted as a vicious cycle to their socio-economic lives.

Case No. 2: Mortgaging Barga Land

Mortgaging barga land in lieu of lump sum money is another transgressing in Barga system now-a-days. Even dangerous side of this anomaly is sometimes not to keep written evidence or giving verbal mortgage of lands. The Bargadars mortgage their land in exchange of money to the third party with or without written contract. The cause of mortgaging as found from the study area is mainly for medical treatment of any family members or for fulfilling the need of the cost of daughter's marriage.

A. Verbal Contract

Two types of contracts have been observed in verbal contract.

(i) The creditor will cultivate the mortgaged barga land and after repayment of loan by the Bargadar, the creditor will return back the land to the Bargadar. At this time the actual landowner remains deprived from his share of produce. This type of anomaly has been observed among marginal Scheduled Caste Bargadars of Birbhum and small Scheduled Caste and semi-medium Muslim Bargadars of Burdwan.

(ii) The creditor will cultivate the mortgaged Barga land for a fixed period of time and after that period he will return back the land to the Bargadar. In this arrangement the Bargadar will not have to repay any loan amount to the creditor. Here also the actual landowner becomes victimised in respect of his share of produce. This type of anomaly has been observed among small Muslim Bargadars of Birbhum District only.

B. Written Contract

Here also two types of contracts have been observed.

(i) A contract is made wherein it is decided that the Bargadar should have to work as daily labour in the house of the creditor until and unless the loan is repaid. The Bargadar also has to mortgage the land and land record (*parcha*) to the creditor for this purpose. The condition is such that if within the fixed time period the loan is not repaid, then the right on produce of the Bargadar's land will be transferred to the party. This whole contract is laid down in black and white duly signed by the Bargadar, creditor and two witnesses from each side on a stamp paper. No political interference has been allowed in this case. This type of anomaly has been observed among semi-medium Muslim Bargadars of Birbhum district. The written script of the mortgage contract is as follows:

> *I am giving loan of Rs __________ to Sri ______________ @ interest _________. If the person cannot repay Rs __________ within ________________ years then I will take the possession of this Barga land. He may repay the loan amount within the fixed period by engaging himself as labour in my agricultural land.*

(ii) The creditor will cultivate the mortgaged Barga land for a fixed period of time and after that period he will return back the land to the bargadar. In this arrangement the Bargadar will not have to repay any loan amount to the creditor. Within this time period, the actual landowner remains deprived from his share of produce. This type of anomaly can be observed among marginal Muslim and small Scheduled Caste Bargadars of Bribhum District. The written script of the mortgaged contract is as follows:

I shall reap the harvest of the crops for earmarked land from the year ________ to the year ________. I am giving sum of Rs __________ to Sri ____________ as a payment of the crops and after ______________ years I shall be obliged to back the land.

These sections of Bargadars should be convicted under the following sections:

Section 17 (I) that the authority appointed by State Government can terminate the cultivation right of Bargadar if:

- The Bargadar has without any reasonable cause failed to cultivate the land or has used if for any purpose other than agriculture.
- The land is not cultivated by the Bargadar personally.
- The bargadar has failed to tender deposit to the full extent the share of the produce as required by sub-section (2) or sub-section (40) as the case may be of section 16 to the land owner.
- That the person (having less than 3 hectares of land) owning the land requires it bona fide for bringing it under personal cultivation.

Section – 20B: Surrender or abandonment by bargadar—

1. If a bargadar –
   (a) Surrender his right to cultivate in relation to any land cultivated by him as a bargadar, or
   (b) Voluntarily abandons cultivation of such land [to the owner of the land or the bargadar or any other person] may give information in written of such surrender or abandonment to the officer or authority appointed under sub section (1) of section 18, having jurisdiction in the area in which such land is situated.
2. On receipt of such information [or on his own motion] such officer or authority shall issue a notice, in the prescribed form to the bargadar and after giving the bargadar and the person whose land was cultivated by

the bargadar, an opportunity of being heard and making such inquiries as he or it may deem necessary determine whether the bargadar voluntarily surrendered or abandoned his right of cultivation in relation to such land.

3. If such officer or authority determines that the bargadar had not voluntarily surrendered or abandoned the cultivation of the land which was being cultivated by him as such and that he had been compelled by force or otherwise to surrender or abandon the cultivation of such land, such officer or authority shall restore the bargadar to the cultivation of the land, or where the bargadar is not available or is not willing to be restored to the cultivation of such land, the person whose land was so cultivated shall not resume personal cultivation of the land, but he may, with the permission of such officer or authority, get the land cultivated by any person, referred to in section 49, who is willing to cultivate the land as a bargadar.
4. If such officer or authority determines that the bargadar had voluntarily surrendered or abandoned the cultivation of the land which was cultivated by him as such, the person whose land was being so cultivated shall not resume personal cultivation of such land but he may, with the permission of such officer or authority, have the land cultivated by any person, referred to in section 49, who is willing to cultivate the land as a bargadar.
5. Any contravention of the provisions of sub-section (3) or sub-section (4) shall be an offence punishable with imprisonment for a term which may extend to six months or with fine which may extend to one thousand rupees, or with both.

Section 16(2) –

The bargadar shall tender, within the prescribed period (within 7 days after threshing) to the person whose land he cultivates, the share of produce due to such person.

Section 18(3) –

The decision of any dispute in clause (a) of subsection (1) [i.e. division or delivery of the produce] shall specify the money value of the share of the produce to be delivered, which shall be payable in default of delivery of such share.

Table 22A: Distribution of Bargadars under Case No. (2) in Birbhum

Operational Land Holding Category (in Acre)	*Ethnic Groups*					
	GC	*SC*	*ST*	*M*	*Total*	*Total Land*
Marginal		3		3	6	5.73
Small		1		1	2	2.94
Semi-Medium				1	1	2.88
Medium						
Large						
Total		4		5	9	11.55

In Birbhum under this case a total of 9 bargadars have been traced out who are holding 11.55 acres of barga land. Here, the majority (66.67%) of the bargadars belong to the marginal categories, who are holding the maximum (54.49%) land out of total barga land comes under this type of violation. In terms of ethnic composition, the bargadars under such case belong to only Scheduled Caste and Muslim communities (Table 22A).

Table 22B: Distribution of Bargadars under Case No. (2) in Burdwan

Operational Land Holding Category (in Acre)	*Ethnic Groups*					*Total Land*	*Owned Land*	*Lease in Land*
	GC	*SC*	*ST*	*M*	*Total*			
Marginal		1			1	0.88	.63	.25
Small								
Semi-Medium				1	1	2.56	2.11	.45
Medium								
Large								
Total		1		1	2	3.44	2.74	0.70

In Burdwan, under such case only two Bargadars have been observed one from Scheduled Caste marginal farmer and another from Muslim semi-medium farmer. They are holding an amount of 3.44 acres of land out of which 2.74 acres are owned and only 0.70 acre is barga (leased in) land.

Table 22C: Distribution of Bargadars under Case No. (2) in Jalpaiguri

Operational Land Holding Category (in Acre)	*GC*	*SC*	*ST*	*M*	*Total*	*Total Land (in Acre)*
Marginal	2	5	3	2	12	2.28
Small	–	–	1	–	1	1.03
Semi-Medium	–	–	–	–	–	–
Medium	–	–	–	–	–	–
Large	–	–	–	–	–	–
Total	2	5	4	2	13	3.31

The maximum number of cases have been found in Jalpaiguri and from all ethnic groups. Though the number is high under such cases, the total land is meager and holding only 3.31 acres of Barga land. Here the majority of the Bargadars are marginal farmers (Table 22C).

Table 23: Demographic Features of the sample Bargadar under Case No. (2)

(*Average per HH*)

District	*Land Category*	*Family Member*	*Literacy Status (except 0-6 years)*	
			Literate	*Illiterate*
Birbhum	Marginal	8.33	1.25	5.09
	Small	8	2.5	3.5
	Semi-medium	7	3	3
Burdwan	Marginal	7	2	3
	Semi-medium	7	3	4
Jalpaiguir	Marginal	5.25	0.42	4.25
	Small	4.00	–	4

The Bargadars fall under such case (no. 2) are mostly illiterate and have large family size. The illiterate farmers who are responsible to feed a large number of mouths are forced to mortgage their only lands (i.e. Barga) to the big landowners (not to the actual land owner of the Barga lands) (Table 23).

From Table 24, it has also been observed that their family's dependency ratio is very high. Very few of the family members are engaged in the occupation like Agriculture/Daily labour in Birbhum whereas in Burdwan except one of marginal Bargadar (who is engaged in service) other family members of all other categories are unemployed. After mortgaging the barga land no marginal bargadars of Birbhum have their cultivable land, so they have changed their occupation from cultivation to Agricultural/ Daily labour

Table 24: Occupational Status of the Sample Bargadars under Case No. (2)

(Average per Household)

District	*Land Category*	*Economic Status*		*Primary Occupation*			*Subsidiary Occupation*	
		Earner	*Dependent*	*Cultivation*	*Service*	*Agri/Daily Labour*	*Agri/Daily Labour*	*Business*
Birbhum	Marginal	1.33	7	–	–	1.33	–	0.66
	Small	2.5	5.5	1	–	1.5	1	0.50
	Semi-medium	2	5	1	–	1	1	–
Burdwan	Marginal	2	5	1	1	–	–	–
	Semi-medium	1	6	1	–	–	–	–
Jalpaiguri	Marginal	1.5	3.75	–	–	1.5	1	–
	Small	2	2	1	–	1	1	–

Table 25: Land Situation of the Sample Bargadars under Case No. (2)

(Average per household in Acre)

District	*Land Category*	*In the Past*			*At Present*		
		Owned	*Leased in*	*Total*	*Owned*	*Leased in*	*Total*
Birbhum	Marginal	–	0.96	0.96	–	–	–
	Samll	–	1.47	1.47	–	0.41	0.41
	Semi-medium	–	2.88	2.88	–	2.88	2.88
Burdwan	Marginal	0.63	0.25	0.88	0.63	–	0.63
	Semi-medium	2.11	0.45	2.56	2.11	–	2.11
Jalpaiguri	Marginal	–	0.19	0.19	–	–	–
	Samll	–	1.03	1.03	–	0.33	–.33

Main subsistence source of Birbhum Bargadars was Barga land. After mortgaging the land, the marginal Bargadars have no cultivable lands and the small Bargadars have very little amount of cultivable lands. The semi-medium Bargadars are cultivating the same amount of land as was in the past because they could repay the loan amount in cash and as a security the creditor has taken the land *parcha* as mortgage. In Burdwan all the bargadars have their owned lands. They have mortgaged their leased in land only. Presently they are cultivating their owned lands and thus avoiding the curse of landlessness (Table 25).

From Table 26, it is seen that the marginal and small farmers of Birbhum and Jalpaiguri are the worst victims of such mortgaging affairs. Their surplus over expenditure shows negative amount and thus proves that they have nothing in their hands to invest on their agriculture what to speak of their emergency cases in future. Others could manage with their positive (though meagre) surplus but the inclination towards landlessness cannot be avoided. It has been traced out that all the bargadars have mortgaged their lands due to accidental need for fulfilling family demand like daughter's marriage and treatment of diseases. An interesting picture has been observed among the semi-medium Muslim Bargadars of Birbhum. They have mortgaged the land but the land is under their self-possession. They are repaying the loan from the wage of their engagement as agricultural labourer in the house of the creditors. But the matter of concern is that the income from the same agricultural land has decreased after mortgaging the land. As these cultivators are compelled to work as agricultural labours in the house of the creditor to repay the loan, they cannot operate their agricultural operations properly and timely. For this their production as well as income is deteriorating.

Case No. 3: Selling out Barga Land

This section of Bargadars has sold out their barga land either to their landowner or to some third party via their landowners. This is due to their inability to cultivate the land for lack of money or due to need of money for emergency purpose. These exchanges have been made either through written document or through verbal commitment. In both the cases the buyer is either the landowner or a third party.

Table 26: Economic Status of the Sample Bargadars under Case No. (2)

(Average per household in Rs.)

District	Land Category	In the Past (Annual)					At Present (Annual)				
		From Agricultural		Total Income Expenditure Status			From Agricultural		Total Income Expenditure Status		
		Income	Expenditure	Income	Expenditure	Surplus	Income	Expenditure	Income	Expenditure	Surplus
Birbhum	Marginal	7966.08	1889.50	12340.00	12398.67	-58.67	-	-	9541.50	9836.17	-294.67
	Small	12667.45	2877.05	18343.12	1792115	421.97	3407.00	827.00	11103.00	11697.50	-594.50
	Semi-medium	22908.00	7856.90	26128.00	24011.80	2116.20	19962.00	6718.65	22862.00	22137.50	724.50
Burdwan	Marginal	18641.60	5188.40	22125.00	21811.50	313.50	16430.00	12060.80	48495.00	38613.75	9881.25
	Semi-medium	56289.70	31560.30	56289.70	54013.00	2276.7	46395.00	26012.59	46395.00	45918.20	476.80
Jalpaiguri	Marginal	1125.50	391.79	5285.50	5416.80	-131.30	-	-	4829.00	5337.65	-508.65
	Small	6216.80	2167.00	9869.00	9952.00	-83	1887.90	638.00	8123.50	8567.50	-443.50

A. Through Written Document

(i) **To Landowner:** These Bargadars have been compelled to sell out their barga land to the landowners by accepting some amount of money or some amount of land. As most of the cases, the Bargadars were the *Mahinders* [day labours in the household of landowner] and at some time the landowners had allowed them to cultivate some acres of land. After the initiation of Operation Barga the labourers had registered the land as barga land in their names. Very often as a feedback, the landowners discharged the labourers from their household and the labourers have to cultivate the barga lands without getting any assistance from the landowners. Hence, the labourers who had converted to Bargadars could hardly stride across the path of cost intensive cultivation. This has been found especially in the Birbhum Bargadars, after a certain time the Bargadars gave up their operations. Having no income generating way, they at a point of time, became compelled to sell out their Barga lands in a nominal rate or in exchange of certain amount to the landowners by giving a written commitment on plain paper that they will not claim the land again. Although, it has no legal-stand and the papers have not been registered anyway. This type of transgression can be observed among semi-medium Scheduled Caste, Scheduled Tribe and Muslim Bargadars of Birbhum.

But in case of Burdwan Bargadars, after a certain time of Barga recording they sold out the land to the landowners in exchange of a lump sum amount of money or some amount of land for being set free from the bitter relationship with landowners. This type of transgression has been observed among the small General Caste and Muslim Bargadars of Burdwan.

(ii) **Via Landowner to the Third Party**: In this case, the landowners offered the Bargadars a lump sum amount for disposing of the lands to the third party. At the time of consignment, the Bargadar signed in an internal written contract promising not to claim the land at any time. After that the landowners sold out the land to some third parties and at the time of 2nd consignment the Bargadars again had to sign in the paper as a witness of selling of land to the third parties in front of the sub-Registrar of Land. This type of incongruity has been observed among the small Scheduled Caste and Muslim Bargadars of Burdwan.

(iii) **By Landowner to Third Party:** It is frequent that the absentee landlords (who resides outside the village) are often deprived from the produce of their lands by the Bargadars, the landowners try to sell out their barga lands to any third party (mostly to one who is residential and also influential). The Bargadar then is liable to submit his shares to the new owner. This type of abnormality has been observed among the large Muslim Bargadars of Birbhum district.

B. Through Verbal Commitment

(i) **To the Landowner:** These sections of Bargadars were the *Mahinders* (daily labourers in the household of landowner) and at that time the landowners allowed them to cultivate some acres of land as sharecroppers. After initiation of Operation Barga, these labourers registered the cultivated lands in their names as barga land. At any point of time, seeing their inability to cultivate the land, the landowners offered a lumpsum amount of money for giving up the rights of barga land. The offer if accepted by the Bargadars the process starts. But the entire process remained as verbal commitment. This inconsistency has been observed among the small Bargadars of Burdwan district.

(ii) **Via Landowner to the Third Party:** In case of emergencies on the part of owners, the landowners offer their Bargadars to purchase the total amount of their Barga land (knowing very well that the Bargadar cannot be able to do that). In this situation, the landowners offered the Bargadars a lump sum amount of money for giving up the land rights. The Bargadars accepted the offer and then the landowners sold the land to the third party. Verbally the Bargadars promised that they would not claim the land for cultivation in future. This anomaly has been observed among the small General Caste Bargadars of Burdwan District.

This section of Bargadars should be convicted under the following sections of West Bangal Land Reforms Act – 1955.

Section 20B: Surrender or abandonment by bargadar –

- If a bargadar –
  - Surrender his right to cultivate in relation to any land cultivated by him as a Bargadar, or
  - Voluntarily abondons cultivation of such land [to the owner of the land or the Bargadar or any other person] may give information in written of such surrender or abandonment to the officer or authority appointed under sub section (1) of section 18, having jurisdiction in the area in which such land is situated.
- On receipt of such information [or on his own motion] such officer or authority shall issue a notice, in the prescribed form to the Bargadar and after giving the Bargadar and the person whose land was cultivated by the Bargadar, an opportunity of being heard and making such inquiries as he or it may deem necessary determine whether the Bargadar voluntarily surrendered or abandoned his right of cultivation in relation to such land.
- If such officer or authority determines that the Bargadar had not voluntarily surrendered or abandoned the cultivation of the land which was being cultivated by him as such and that he had been compelled by force or otherwise to surrender or abandon the cultivation of such land, such officer or authority shall restore the bargadar to the cultivation of the land, or where the bargadar is not available or is not willing to be restored to the cultivation of such land, the person whose land was so cultivated shall not resume personal cultivation of the land, but he may, with the permission of such officer or authority, get the land cultivated by any person, referred to in section – 49, who is willing to cultivate the land as a Bargadar.
- If such officer or authority determines that the Bargadar had voluntarily surrendered or abandoned the cultivation of the land which was cultivated by him as such, the person whose land was being so cultivated shall not resume personal cultivation of such land but he may, with the

permission of such officer or authority, have the land cultivated by any person, referred to in section 49, who is willing to cultivate the land as a Bargadar.

- Any contravention of the provisions of sub-section (3) or sub-section (4) shall be an offence punishable with imprisonment for a term, which may extend to six months or with fine, which may extend to one thousand rupees, or with both.

Section 16(2) –

The bargadar shall tender, within the prescribed period (within 7 days after threshing) to the person whose land he cultivates, the share of produce due to such person.

Section 18(3) –

The decision of any dispute in clause (a) of sub-section (1) [i.e. division or delivery of the produce] shall specify the money value of the share of the produce to be delivered, which shall be payable in default of delivery of such share.

Table 27A: Distribution of Bargadars under Case No. (3) in Birbhum

Operational Land Holding Category (in Acre)	*Ethnic Groups*					*Total land*
	GC	*SC*	*ST*	*M*	*Total*	
Marginal						
Small						
Semi-medium		1	1	1	3	8.13
Medium		–	–	1	1	3.31
Large		–	–	2	2	8.06
Total		1	1	4	6	19.50

In Birbhum under this case, 6 bargadars have been traced out who are holding total 19.50 acres of barga land. They have no owned land. Among them 50 per cent belong to the Semi-Medium farmer group but the maximum lands (0.41%) are in the hands of large farmer groups (Table 27A).

In Burdwan under this case a total of 9 Bargadars have been observed who are holding 14.31 acres of land out of which 11.07 acres are owned land and 3.24 acres are barga lands. All the Bargadars are small farmers (Table 27B).

Table 27B: Distribution of Bargadars under Case No. (3) in Burdwan

Operational Land Holding Category (in Acre)	*Ethnic Groups*				*Total*	*Total Land (in Acre)*	*Owned Land*	*Leased in Land*
	GC	*SC*	*ST*	*M*				
Marginal								
Small	3	2	–	4	9	14.31	11.07	3.24
Semi-medium								
Medium								
Large								
Total	3	2		4	9	14.31	11.07	3.24

Table 27C: Distribution of Bargadars under Case No. (3) in Jalpaiguri

Operational Land Holding Categories (in Acre)	*GC*	*SC*	*ST*	*M*	*Total*	*Total Land (in Acre)*
Marginal	2	–	2	2	6	1.40
Small	2	7	5	–	14	16.05
Semi-medium	–	–	–	–	–	–
Medium	–	2	–	–	2	7.66
Large	–	2	3	–	5	22.54
Total	4	11	10	2	27	47.65

In Jalpaiguri 27 Bargadars have been traced out who are holding total 47.65 acres of barga land. They have no owned land. Among them majority belong to Small farmer groups. But maximum land holding is in the hands of Large Bargadars.

Table 28: Demographic feature of the Sample Households under Case No. (3)

(Average per Household)

District	*Land Category*	*Family Member*	*Literacy Status (except 0-6 years)*	
			Literate	*Illiterate*
Birbhum	Semi-medium	9.66	2	5
	Medium	13	1	8
	Large	11	2	6
Burdwan	Small	6	2.55	2.45
Jalpaiguri	Marginal	6.33	0.83	4.66
	Small	6.21	0.64	4.21
	Medium	5.00	–	4.00
	Large	6.60	–	5.40

Dependency ratio is very high in all three districts. The literacy rates are also bleak in all three districts (Table 28 & 29). In Birbhum it is found that all the Semi-medium and Medium bargadars have adopted the Agricultural or Daily labour activities as their subsidiary occupations for mitigating their family needs. Whereas in Burdwan very few have adopted this occupation as most of them cannot get any extra time after cultivation for engaging themselves in subsidiary occupation. In Jalpaiguri, Small and Semi-medium farmers opted their subsidiary occupations as daily labours or agricultural labours.

Table 29: Occupational Status of Sample Households under Case No. (3)

(Average per Household)

District	*Land Category*	*Economic Status*		*Primary Occupation*				*Subsidiary Occupation*
		Earner	*Dependent*	*Cultivation*	*Business*	*Service*	*Agri/Daily Labour*	*Agri/Daily Labour*
Birbhum	Semi-medium	2.66	7	1	0.66	–	1	1
	Medium	2	11	1	–	–	1	1
	Large	2	9	1	–	–	1	–
Burdwan	Small	2	4	1	0.55	0.22	0.22	0.22
Jalpaiguri	Marginal	1.33	5.00	–	–	1.33	–	–
	Small	1.28	4.93	–	–	1.28	–	0.14
	Medium	1.00	4.00	1	–	–	0.5	0.5
	Large	1.60	5.00	1	0.60	–	–	–

Before selling out their barga lands, the Bargadars of Birbhum had no owned land. But after selling their barga land, they are cultivating only owned land (which they have acquired from their landlords as a share by disposing of their barga lands). In case of Burdwan the picture is different. Like most of the Birbhum Bargadars they are not accepting the land as a share while disposing of their barga lands. They preferred to get a lump sum amount from landowner in stead of getting meager amount of land. In Jalpaiguri no marginal and small Bargadar have land for cultivation. They are engaged in Agriculture and or Daily Labour activities. After selling out their barga lands, the Marginal and Small farmers of Jalpaiguri district have nothing to cultivate. They became landless labourers from landed Bargadars (Table 30).

Table 30: Land Situation of the Sample Bargadars under Case No. (3)

(Average per Household in Acre)

District	*Land Category*	*In the Past*			*At Present*		
		Owned	*Leased in*	*Total*	*Owned*	*Leased in*	*Total*
Birbhum	Semi-medium	–	2.71	2.71	1.23	–	1.23
	Medium	–	3.31	3.31	1.11	–	1.11
	Large	–	4.03	4.03	1.93	0.26	2.19
Burdwan	Small	1.23	0.36	1.59	1.23	0.10	1.33
Jalpaiguri	Marginal	–	0.23	0.23	–	–	–
	Small	–	1.15	1.15	–	–	–
	Medium	–	3.83	3.83	1.5	–	1.5
	Large	–	4.51	4.51	1.06	1.33	2.39

The marginally positive surplus over expenditure at past and negative surplus at present time of Birbhum Bargadars clearly indicates that after selling out the land (which were their only source of subsistence) their income has deteriorated in such a way that they are unable to subsist on it only. And as a result they are in debt trap throughout the year at present. Before selling out the land their surplus was too meager to mitigate their emergency need of capital, as a result they were compelled to sell out their lands. In Burdwan, the situation of very few Bargadars is alike Birbhum Bargadars, but in most of the cases they had and have their owned land. Their surplus ratio was better and even at present their surplus is marginally positive. Actually they have sold out the land on the one hand to minimize the bitter relationship with their landlords and on the other hand for their greed of lump sum amount of money. In case of Jalpaiguri Bargadars, except Small farmers, other two categories have their surplus of expenditures positive at present after selling out their barga lands (Table 31).

Table 31: Economic Status of the Sample Households under Case No. (3)

(Average per household in Rs.)

District	Land Category	In the Past (Annual)					At Present (Annual)				
		From Agriculture		Total Income Expenditure Status			From Agriculture		Total Income Expenditure Status		
		Income	Expenditure	Income	Expenditure	Surplus	Income	Expenditure	Income	Expenditure	Surplus
Birbhum	Semi-medium	22829.50	5775.00	28138.83	26946.42	1192.41	11361.55	2921.13	17537.80	17991.20	-453.40
	Medium	31142.00	8170.80	36928.00	36909.85	18.15	11443.00	2706.70	17443.00	17621.90	-178.9
	Large	38966.90	10142.50	40366.90	39340.20	1026.70	20175.70	5811.40	24175.70	24721.00	-545.30
Burdwan	Small	38178.17	17808.37	53663.35	48164.83	5498.52	30935	14189.30	46420.18	45402.27	1017.91
Jalpaiguri	Marginal	1243.30	436.00	7895.50	8516.75	-621.25	–	–	6918.45	7806.60	-825.15
	Small	6976.05	2513.15	10846.40	11109.70	-263.30	–	–	6613.80	7245.10	-631.30
	Medium	23164.00	7698.50	30081.70	23570.00	6511.70	9925.50	3161.50	19148.50	20016.25	-867.75
	Large	28194.20	9311.60	36721.00	27037.55	9683.45	15178.60	5040.50	33579.60	25193.70	8385.90

Case No. 4: Political Eviction

Unscrupulous political eviction in favour of political party men (who are landowners also) is very common in the district of Birbhum. Without any justification and banking on any loopholes of any kind, the influential party men evict the legitimate claimants with the help of local panchayats. This type of irregularity has been observed in case of Large Scheduled Caste Bargadars of Birbhum district.

The landowner should be convicted as his activity is going against the statement mentioned in Section 17 and Section 15 (1) under West Bengal Land Reforms Act, 1956.

West Bengal Land Reforms (Bargadar) Rules, 1956 has kept a provision under section 17 (I) that the authority appointed by State Government can only terminate the cultivation right of Bargadar if:

- The Bargadar has without any reasonable cause failed to cultivate the land or has used it for any purpose other than agriculture.
- The land is not cultivated by the Bargadar personally.
- The bargadar has failed to tender deposit to the full extent of the share of the produce as required by sub-section – (2) or sub-section (40) as the case may be of section 16 to the landowner.
- That the person (having less than 3 hectares of land) owning the land requires it bona fide for bringing it under personal cultivation.

Again Section 15 states in sub-sections that:

- The provisions of clauses (b) and (c) of sub-section (4) of section 4 shall not apply to the holding of a raiyat or any part of it which is cultivated by a bargadar so long as cultivation by a bargadar continues.
- The right of cultivation of land by bargadar shall be heritable and shall not be transferable.

This anomaly has been observed in Birbhum District only. One Scheduled Caste Large Bargadar has been traced out in the study area, whose operational barga holding was 4.07 acres (Table 32).

Table 32: Distribution of Bargadars as per Ethnicity under Case No. (4) in Birbhum

Operational Land Holding Category (in Acre)	*GC*	*SC*	*ST*	*M*	*Total*	*Total Land (in Acre)*
Marginal						
Small						
Semi-medium						
Medium						
Large		1			1	4.07
Total		1			1	4.07

The family size of the Bargadar is more than average and most of the family members are illiterate (Table 33).

Table 33: Demographic Features of the Sample Household under Case No. (4)

(Average per Household)

District	*Land Category*	*Family Member*	*Literacy Status (except 0-6 years)*	
			Literate	*Illiterate*
Birbhum	Large	6	2	4

Only two earning members feed the entire family. Primary occupation of the Bargadar is cultivation and presently his son started vegetable vending finds no alternative in agriculture. The land they cultivate will certainly insufficient to provide full employment to him and his father. They have no subsidiary occupation (Table 34).

Table 34: Occupational Status of Sample Household under Case No. (4)

(Average per Household)

District	*Land Category*	*Economic Status*		*Primary Occupation*		*Subsidiary Occupation*
		Earner	*Dependant*	*Cultivation*	*Business*	*Agri/Daily Labour*
Birbhum	Large	2	4	1	1	-

The Bargadar could manage his subsistence from his barga lands. But after the incidence of political eviction from some portion of his barga lands, the amount of barga land came down to almost half (Table 35).

Table 35: Land Situation of the Sample Bargadars under Case No. (4)

(in Acres)

District	*Land Category*	*In the Past*			*At Present*		
		Owned	*Leased in*	*Total*	*Owned*	*Leased in*	*Total*
Birbhum	Large	–	4.07	4.07	–	2.97	2.97

His agricultural support system (Table 36) is somehow better than other farmers. He used the machineries for better and intensive cultivation. But at present he is in problem with the machineries, as they should be used optimally to achieve optimal production from an optimal land size.

Table 36: Agricultural Support System of the Sample Households under Case No. (4)

District	*Land Category*	*Household having (in number)*					
		Bullock Cart	*Plough & Bullock*	*Sprayer*	*Thresher*	*Shallow Tube well/ Submersible*	*Tractor/ Power tiller*
Birbhum	Large	1	1	1	-	-	-

Table 37: Economic Status of the Sample Households under Case No. (4)

(Average per Household in Rs.)

District	*Land Category*	*In the Past (Annual)*					*At Present (Annual)*				
		From Agriculture		*Total Income Expenditure Status*			*From Agriculture*		*Total Income Expenditure Status*		
		Income	*Expenditure*	*Income*	*Expenditure*	*Surplus*	*Income*	*Expenditure*	*Income*	*Expenditure*	*Surplus*
Birbhum	Large	41778.00	12854.60	44916.00	38667.45	6248.55	28437.70	8942.50	31575.70	31560.10	15.60

Previously the surplus over expenditure of the Bargadar was better (Table 37), which clearly indicates that his income from agriculture and also from other sources was sufficient to mitigate his family need including agriculture expenses. But after political eviction his surplus has drastically come down. As the area is too much backward, so he became unable to find out some other jobs for supplementing the slashed off expenditures. The picture evidently projects that after certain years he will be unable to invest required amount on agriculture and his economic condition will be no longer sustainable.

Case No. 5: Forceful Acquisition of Barga Land by Landowners

It is happening in the cases where for several years the Bargadar has not given any share of the produce to the landowner. The forceful acquisition has been performed with the active support of the local political party and with the help of the panchayat members.

Table 38A: Distribution of Bargadar under Case No. (5) in Birbhum

Operational Land Holding Category (in Acre)	*Ethnic Groups*				*Total*	*Total Land (acres)*
	GC	*SC*	*ST*	*M*		
Marginal						
Small						
Semi-medium						
Medium						
Large				1	1	4.09
Total				1	1	4.09

Table 38B: Distribution of Bargadars under Case No. (5) in Jalpaiguri

Operational Land Holding Category (in Acre)	*Ethnic Groups*				*Total*	*Total Land (acres)*
	GC	*SC*	*ST*	*M*		
Marginal						
Small						
Semi-medium		1			1	2.21
Medium			2		2	7.50
Large						
Total		1	2		3	9.71

This section of Bargadars has been observed in Birbhum and Jalpaiguri districts. The Birbhum Bargadar falls under large farmer category but in Jalpaiguri the cases are found among Semi-medium and Medium categories of farmers (Tables 38A & 38B).

Table 39: Demographic features of the Sample Households under Case No. (5)

District	*Land Category*	*Average Total Family Member*	*Literacy Status (except 0-6 years)*	
			Literate	*Illiterate*
Birbhum	Large	5	-	4
Jalpaiguri	Semi-medium	7	1	6
	Medium	5.5	1	4

It is found from Table 39 that the illiteracy is prevalent among the Bargadars of such cases in both the districts. Dependency ratio of these families is also very high (Table 40). In Birbhum, the Bargadar (the head of the household) was the only source of income. After forceful acquisition of his barga land he has adopted the occupation of Agricultural labour primarily and subsidiarily has engaged himself in Business (as a Hawker in off season).

Table 40: Occupational Status of Sample Bargadars under Case No. (5)

District	*Land Category*	*Economic Status*		*Primary Occupation*		*Subsidiary Occupation*
		Earner	*Dependent*	*Cultivation*	*Agri/Daily Labour*	*Business*
Birbhum	Large	1	4	–	1	1
Jalpaiguri	Semi-medium	2	5	–	2	1
	Medium	2	3.5	–	2	–

In all cases, it has been found that after forceful acquisition of barga lands; no Bargadar possesses any land for their future operations (Table 41). Therefore, all Bargadars have compelled to shift to new occupations like agriculture and or daily labours.

Table 41: Land Situation of the Sample Bargadars under Case No. (5)

(In acres)

District	*Land Category*	*In the Past*			*At Present*		
		Owned	*Leased in*	*Total*	*Owned*	*Leased in*	*Total*
Birbhum	Large	–	4.09	4.09	–	–	–
Jalpaiguri	Semi-medium	–	2.21	2.21	–	–	–
	Medium	–	3.75	3.75	–	–	–

Before forceful acquisition of barga land by the owners, the income from agriculture was positive for the Bargadars. They could manage to live with that income with some stray activities as supplementary source of income. But, after acquisition of land by owners the surplus has come down sharply (Table 42). Virtually *no surplus situation*, compels them to act as daily or agricultural labours in other's field.

Table 42: Economic Status of the Sample Bargadars under Case No. (5)

(Average per Household in Rs.)

District	*Land Category*	*In the Past (Annual)*					*At Present (Annual)*				
		From Agriculture		*Total Income Expenditure Status*			*From Agriculture*		*Total Income Expenditure Status*		
		Income	*Expenditure*	*Income*	*Expenditure*	*Surplus*	*Income*	*Expenditure*	*Income*	*Expenditure*	*Surplus*
Birbhum	Large	35110.70	9982.15	37690.70	33138.55	4552.15	–	–	9842.00	10267.30	-425.30
Jalpaiguri	Semi-medium	12763.00	4675.00	16156.00	15921.00	235	–	–	8748.00	9089.50	-341.50
	Medium	21691.50	7892.00	23812.00	18096.00	5716	–	–	7010.00	7915.35	-905.35

Case No. 6: Cultivating Barga Land Through Mutual Understanding

As the Bargadar was unable to deposit the share of the produce to the landowner, both of them made a verbal contract wherein the land was divided into two equal halves to be cultivated by both of them by their own self and so there would be no liability and responsibility of both the parties towards each other. This type of anomaly has been observed in case of large Scheduled Caste Bargadars of Birbhum, Marginal Muslim Bargadars of Burdwan and Semi-medium, Medium and Large categories of farmers of all communities in Jalpaiguri district.

Both the Landowners and Bargadars are violating sections 15 and 17 of Land Reforms Act, 1956 as given earlier.

Table 43A: Distribution of Bargadars under Case No. (6) in Birbhum

Operational Land Holding Category (in Acre)	*Ethnic Groups*				*Total*	*Total Land*
	GC	*SC*	*ST*	*M*		
Marginal						
Small						
Semi-medium						
Medium						
Large		1			1	4.12
Total		1			1	4.12

In Birbhum, this anomaly has been observed in only one Scheduled Caste Bargadar who possesses 4.12 acres of barga land on his account (Table 43A). Whereas in Burdwan it has been observed in the Marginal Muslim Bargadar. He has no owned land and possesses 0.92 acre of Barga land (Table 43B).

Table 43B: Distribution of Bargadars under Case No. (6) in Burdwan

Operational Land Holding Category (in Acre)	*GC*	*SC*	*ST*	*M*	*Total*	*Total Land*	*Owned Land*	*Leased in Land*
Marginal				1	1	0.92	-	0.92
Small								
Semi-medium								
Medium								
Large								
Total				1	1	0.92	-	0.92

The anomalies are profound in Jalpaiguri and all the ethnic groups having such anomalies starting from Semi-medium Bargadars to Large one. None of these farmers have their own operational holdings except their recorded barga lands. Altogether they cultivate 159.58 acres of barga land (Table 43C). Therefore, according to the mutual contract only 50 per cent out of these total lands are being cultivated by the actual Bargadars. The respective landowners operate the rest of the lands.

Table 43C: Distribution of Bargadars under Case No. (6) in Jalpaiguri

Operational Land Holding Category (in Acre)	*GC*	*SC*	*ST*	*M*	*Total*	*Total Land (in Acre)*
Marginal	-	-	-	-	-	-
Small	-	-	-	-	-	-
Semi-medium	1	1	-	-	2	5.02
Medium	1	4	4	-	9	34.29
Large	1	8	12	2	23	120.27
Total	3	13	16	2	34	159.58

The family size of Birbhum bargadar is very high than the other categories of Bargadars in other two districts. Though the literacy level of all the Bargadars of all the districts are very poor (Table 44).

Table 44: Demographic Features of the Sample Households under Case No. (6)

(Average per Household)

District	*Land Category*	*Family Member*	*Literacy Status (except 0-6 years)*	
			Literate	*Illiterate*
Birbhum	Large	7	2	5
Burdwan	Marginal	3	3	-
Jalpaiguri	Semi-medium	4.5	1	3.5
	Medium	5.11	1.44	3.00
	Large	4.74	1.35	2.69

The dependency ratio is high as usual for all categories of Bargadars. The rate is highest in Birbhum. Though the primary occupations remain cultivation, diversification has been found in occupation. Wherein the dependency ratio is high the diversification of occupation could be found more and more (Table 45).

Table 45: Occupational Status of Sample Bargadars under Case No. (6)

(Average per Household)

District	*Land Category*	*Economic Status*		*Primary Occupation*	*Subsidiary Occupation*
		Earner	*Dependent*	*Cultivation*	*Business*
Birbhum	Large	1	6	1	1
Burdwan	Marginal	1	2	1	1
Jalpaiguri	Semi-medium	1.5	3	1	.5
	Medium	1.78	3.33	1	.78
	Large	1.48	3.26	1	.48

An extraordinary case could be found from Table 46. Before any mutual understanding between the Landowners and the Bargadars, the Bargadars had the rights to operate the entire barga land possessed by them only. But after mutual understanding the Bargadars of all the districts are cultivating the half of their barga land and that has been redesignated as their own lands and the rest of the lands are cultivated by the respective landlords by their own. The Bargadars are cultivating their lands with their own costs and there is no question of share of products between the landowners and the Bargadars.

Table 46: Land Situation of the Sample Bargadars under Case No. (6)

(Average per Household in Acre)

District	*Land Category*	*In the Past*			*At Present*		
		Owned	*Leased in*	*Total*	*Owned*	*Leased in*	*Total*
Birbhum	Large	–	4.12	4.12	2.06	–	2.06
Burdwan	Marginal	–	0.92	0.92	0.46	–	0.46
Jalpaiguri	Semi-medium	–	2.51	2.51	1.27	–	1.27
	Medium	–	3.81	3.81	1.63	–	1.63
	Large	–	5.23	5.23	2.59	–	2.59

If we only consider the cases of Bargadars we could find that before mutual understanding, the surplus over expenditure (cash in hand) of the Bargadars of all three districts were positive and substantial. But after the incidence of mutual contract, the surplus has come down. Even at present the surplus of Birbhum Bargadar shows negative figures. Half the land out of total barga operations could not substantiate their family incomes. Again, as his family size is large and has no other income source, so he has to mitigate his family demand by borrowing money from non-institutional local sources (i.e. from Moneylenders). But in Burdwan and Jalpaiguri districts, though this surplus has decreased yet they are still in the positive side and sufficient cash in hand to operate their families (Table 47).

Case No. 7: Mutual Distribution of Barga Land Between all the heirs after the death of Bargadar

According to Bargadari Act, the succession of any barga land is very difficult after the demise of the Bargadar. But in most of the cases after sudden demise of the Bargadar it is an usual practice to distribute the barga land among the heirs of the deceased. But legally they are not recognized and in major cases the Panchayat and BLLRO office remain totally uninformed and in some cases this is happening with the support of the Panchayat officials. The successors divide the plots into several segments and practice cultivation on barga lands. The other side of the irregularities is that the lands become uneconomic and one cannot operate up to the economies of scale.

This section of Bargadars are violating the section 15A (1) of West Bengal Land Reforms Act, 1956. The law states:

Continuation right of cultivation of the land on the death of the Bargadar: Sub-section (1) of Section 15 (A) makes specific provision as to how the right of cultivation of the land of a Bargadar would continue on the death of the Bargadar. Sub-section (1) shall have effect notwithstanding anything contained in any law for the time being in force or in any contract to the contrary. When the bargadar leaves only one heir, then there will be no problem. Then as soon as the Bargadar dies then such lawful heir of the Bargadar may continue the cultivation of such land. Where, however, there are more than one lawful heirs then such heirs of the Bargadar

Table 47: Economic Status of the Sample Bargadars under Case No. (6)

(Average per Household in Rs.)

District	Land Category	At Past (Annual)					At Present (Annual)				
		From Agriculture		Total Income Expenditure Status			From Agriculture		Total Income Expenditure Status		
		Income	Expenditure	Income	Expenditure	Surplus	Income	Expenditure	Income	Expenditure	Surplus
Birbhum	Large	36260.00	10346.70	41148.00	33931.55	7216.45	16378.50	3993.95	20266.50	20939.50	-673
Burdwan	Marginal	20920.00	7976.60	29920.00	20611.50	9308.50	9970.00	3658.50	19970.00	17681.30	2288.70
Jalpaiguri	Semi-medium	16728.50	7146.80	18921.50	17877.00	1044.50	8486.15	3621.20	14318.50	14158.70	159.80
	Medium	25172.65	10916.09	28006.65	23219.57	4787.08	10769.40	4610.70	18437.95	17967.35	470.60
	Large	3446.05	14721.30	36019.55	25191.38	10828.17	16959.35	7389.27	21307.05	18198.33	3108.72

shall have to determine within the period prescribed who among them shall cultivate the land of the deceased Bargadar. Rule 2A (1) of the West Bengal Land Reforms (Bargadar) Rules, 1956 provides that all lawful heirs of a deceased bargadar have to determine within a period of thirty days from the date of death of the deceased bargadar the lawful heir who may continue the cultivation of such land.

But this rule often violated by the unlawful heirs of the deceased Bargadar. There are cases found in all three districts. In the following tables (48A, 48B and 48C), how the actual Bargadars are distributed ethnically has been depicted one by one.

Table 48A: Distribution of Bargadar Households under Case No. (7) in Birbhum

Operational Land Holding Category (in Acre)	*Ethnic Groups*				*Total*	*Total Land*
	GC	*SC*	*ST*	*M*		
Marginal						
Small		1			1	1.92
Semi-medium	1	2		1	4	11.64
Medium				3	3	11.915
Large						
Total	1	3		4	8	25.475

Table 48B: Distribution of Bargadar Households under Case No. (7) in Burdwan

Operational Land Holding Category (in Acre)	*Ethnic Group*				*Total*	*Total Land*	*Owned Land*	*Leased in Land*
	GC	*SC*	*ST*	*M*				
Marginal		1			1	0.50		0.50
Small								
Semi-medium								
Medium				2	2	6.53	4.99	1.54
Large								
Total		1		2	3	7.03	4.99	2.04

Table 48C: Distribution of Bargadar Households under Case No. (7) in Jalpaiguri

Operational Land Holding Category (in Acre)	*GC*	*SC*	*ST*	*M*	*Total*	*Total Land (in Acre)*
Marginal	-	-	-	-	-	-
Small	-	-	-	-	-	-
Semi-medium	-	-	-	-	-	-
Medium	1	-	1	-	2	7.82
Large	1	1	4	2	8	39.44
Total	2	1	5	2	10	47.26

Under this anomaly, there are 8 cases found in Birbhum, 3 cases found in Burdwan and 10 cases found in Jalpaiguri district. In Birbhum most of the Bargadars were belonged to Semi-medium category, but cases are found among Small and Medium categories also (Table 48A). The Bargadars had no owned lands; their subsistence were totally depended on the production of their barga lands.

In Burdwan total 3 bargadar families have been found who are involved in this transgression. Majority (66.67%) of them belonged to the Medium farmer category and they were holding the maximum lands, out of which 4.99 acres were their owned lands and 1.54 acres were Barga lands. The only one Marginal Bargadar had no owned land; his subsistence was totally depending on Barga land (Table 48B).

In Jalpaiguri this type of anomaly has been observed in 10 cases. Majority of them belonged to the Large farmer category and they were holding maximum amount of land (Table 48C).

Table 49A: Distribution of Heirs of Bargadars under Case No. (7) in Birbhum

Operational Land Holding Category (in Acre)	*Ethnic Groups*				*Total*	*Total Land (in Acre)*
	GC	*SC*	*ST*	*M*		
Marginal	-	3	-	6	9	8.80
Small	2	2	-	4	8	16.675
Total	2	5	-	10	17	25.475

After the death of these Bargadars, all the heirs (i.e. sons) have distributed the total barga land mutually and cultivating their own portions. They are giving the share of produce to the landowner separately.

Table 49B: Distribution of Heirs of Bargadars under Case No. (7) in Burdwan

Operational Land Category (in Acre)	*Ethnic Group*				*Total*	*Land (in Acre)*		
	GC	*SC*	*ST*	*M*		*Total*	*Owned*	*Leased in*
Marginal	-	2	-	-	2	0.50	-	0.50
Small	-	-	-	5	5	6.53	4.99	1.54
Total	-	2	-	5	7	7.03	4.99	2.04

In Birbhum, the barga lands of the deceased 8 Bargadar have been distributed among their 17 heirs. As cultivator groups, the heirs lie under Marginal and Small farmer groups (Table 49A). Similarly in Burdwan, the lands of total 3 bargadars have been distributed among their 7 heirs. They belong to the Marginal and Small farmer categories (Table 49B). In Jalpaiguri the barga lands of 10 deceased Bargadars have been distributed among 29 heirs. They belong to the Small and Medium farmer groups (Table 49C).

Table 49C: Distribution of Heirs of Bargadar under Case No. (7) in Jalpaiguri

Operational Land Holding Category	*GC*	*SC*	*ST*	*M*	*Total*	*Total Land (acres)*
Small	7	-	13	7	27	42.21
Semi-medium	-	2	-	-	2	5.05
Total	7	2	13	7	29	47.26

Average family size of all the Bargadars in all three districts is within the normal range. But .their literacy status remain unchanged like other category Bargadars (Table 50).

Table 50: Demographic Features of the Sample Bargadars under Case No. (7)

(Average per Household)

District	*Land Category*	*Family Member*	*Literacy Status (except 0-6 years)*	
			Literate	*Illiterate*
Birbhum	Marginal	4.89	1.22	2.67
	Small	4.12	1.00	2.38
Burdwan	Marginal	4.00	1.00	3.00
	Small	4.20	2.4	1.4
Jalpaiguri	Small	4.55	1.44	2.29
	Semi-medium	3.00	1	2

The dependency ratio is high among all categories of Bargadars as earner is less than the dependants. Hence, the diversification of occupation occurs in all groups to meet the needs of the teeming members. Though major occupation remains cultivation for the entire sample Bargadars, as subsidiary occupations they have to pledge their physical labours in occasions (Table 51).

Table 51: Occupational Status of Sample Bargadars (Heirs) under Case No. (7)

District	*Land Category*	*Economic Status*		*Primary Occupation*				*Subsidiary Occupation*	
		Earner	*Dependent*	*Cultivation*	*Business*	*Agri/Daily Labour*	*Other*	*Agri/Daily Labour*	*Business*
Birbhum	Marginal	1.66	3.23	1	0.44		0.22	1	0.11
	Small	2.13	1.99	1	0.38	0.75	-	0.50	0.13
Burdwan	Marginal	2	2	1	-	1	-	1	-
	Small	1.80	2.40	1	0.40	0.20	0.20	0.4	-
Jalpaiguri	Small	1.55	3.00	1	0.04	0.33	0.18	-	0.11
	Semi-medium	1.50	1.50	1	-	0.50	-	-	-

From land situation picture (Table 52) of the successors of the deceased Bargadars, it is clear that all the heirs possess uneconomic holding of cultivation. When a gross land is distributed among many members of a family, the fragmentation and subdivision of lands occur simultaneously. Both are harmful for any economic entrepreneurship.

Table 52: Land Situation of the Sample Bargadars (Heirs) under Case No. (7)

(Average per household in Acre)

District	*Land Category*	*Land*		
		Owned	*Leased in*	*Total*
Birbhum	Marginal	–	0.98	0.98
	Small	–	2.08	2.08
Burdwan	Marginal	–	0.25	0.25
	Small	1.00	0.31	1.31
Jalpaiguri	Small	–	1.56	1.56
	Semi-medium	–	2.53	2.53

From their income expenditure statement (Table 53), it is clear that their surplus remains as low as Rs. 300 or even negative. This amount is neither sufficient to run even a one member family, nor it is worthy for reinvestment in agriculture. This gives the signal of being debt trapped under the hands of moneylenders and venture towards landed bargadar to landless agriculture and/or daily labours.

Table 53: Economic Status of the Sample Bargadars under Case No. (7)

(Average per Household in Rs.)

District	*Land Category*	*From Agriculture (Annual)*		*Total Income–Expenditure status (Annual)*		
		Income	*Expenditure*	*Income*	*Expenditure*	*Surplus*
Birbhum	Marginal	9408.22	2460.44	16158.22	15842.33	315.89
	Small	19711.31	5283.50	24239.81	21619.48	2620.33
Burdwan	Marginal	5942.70	1936.45	11942.70	12106.50	-163.80
	Small	21541.15	10585.25	25883.15	24137.56	1745.59
Jalpaiguri	Small	10141.56	4319.07	15961.18	15609.22	351.96
	Semi-medium	16905.46	7301.58	17634.95	16179.50	1455.45

Case No. 8: Use of Barga Land in Non-agricultural Purpose

In this case the Bargadar has built up house using a part of his Barga land. The remaining portion of the land is being cultivated. The landowner resides outside the village and the Bargadar does not give him any share of produce. This anomaly has been observed in case of Marginal Scheduled Caste Bargadar of Burdwan District.

The Bargdars should be convicted and evicted under the clause (a) of Section 17 (5) and Section 16 (2).

Section 17: Termination of cultivation by bargadar –

(1) No person shall be entitled to terminate cultivation of his land by a bargadar except in execution of an order, made by such officer or authority as the State Government may appoint, that (a) the bargadar has without any reasonable cause failed to cultivate the land, or has used if for any purpose other than agriculture.

Section 16(2) –

The bargadar shall tender, within the prescribed period (within 7 days after threshing) to the person whose land he cultivates, the share of produce due to such person.

This anomaly has been observed in Burdwan district only. Only one bargadar has been traced out who is Marginal Scheduled Caste farmer. He has 0.23 acres of barga land under his possession. A portion of such land has been used as house instead of cultivating the entire land (Table 54).

Table 54: Distribution of Barga Household under Case No. (8) in Burdwan

Operational Land Holding Category (in Acre)	*GC*	*SC*	*ST*	*M*	*Total*	*Total Land*	*Owned Land*	*Leased in Land*
Marginal		1			1	0.53	0.30	0.23
Small								
Semi-medium								
Medium								
Large								
Total		1			1	0.53	0.30	0.23

Table 55: Demographic Features of the Sample Bargadar under Case No. (8)

(Average per Household)

District	*Land Category*	*Family Member*	*Literacy Status (except 0-6 years)*	
			Literate	*Illiterate*
Burdwan	Marginal	5	3	2

His family size is large and the literacy rate is high unlike other cases (Table 55). Two out of 5 are earner in his family. The primary occupations of these two are cultivation and business respectively. The dependent members are three. The head of the household himself is engaged in business for his supplementary income and as subsidiary occupation (Table 56).

Table 56: Occupation Status of Sample Bargadars under Case No. (8)

(Average per household)

District	*Land Category*	*Economic Status*		*Primary Occupation*		*Subsidiary Occupation*	
		Earner	*Depen-dent*	*Cultiva-tion*	*Business*	*Agri/Daily Labour*	*Business*
Burdwan	Marginal	2	3	1	1	-	1

Table 57: Land Situation of the Sample Bargadar under Case No. (8)

(Average per Household in Acre)

District	*Land Category*	*In the Past*			*At Present*		
		Owned	*Leased in*	*Total*	*Owned*	*Leased in*	*Total*
Burdwan	Marginal	0.30	0.23	0.53	0.30	0.20	0.50

The Bargadar possesses 0.30 acres of owned land and 0.23 acres of barga land. Before construction of house, he used to cultivate in the total 0.53 acres of land as his operational holding. But after transgression as he has built up his house on 0.03 acres of barga land, now he could hardly cultivate 0.50 acres of land (Table 57).

Except one plough and a pair of bullock, he has no other agricultural support system (machineries and implements). He hires required support system from local market, which is easily available in Burdwan.

Table 58: Economic Status of the Sample Bargadar under Case No. (8)

(Average per Household in Rs.)

District	Land Category	*In the Past (Annual)*					*At Present (Annual)*				
		From Agriculture		*Total Income Expenditure Status*			*From Agriculture*		*Total Income Expenditure Status*		
		Income	*Expenditure*	*Income*	*Expenditure*	*Surplus*	*Income*	*Expenditure*	*Income*	*Expenditure*	*Surplus*
Birbhum	Marginal	18946.20	7842.00	31246.20	27141.90	4104.30	17873.70	7398.10	30173.70	26698.00	3475.70

The surplus over expenditure of the bargadar household shows that it has marginally decreased at present than the past. It is the direct impact of using cultivable land to non-agricultural purposes (Table 58). It is true, that among the sample Bargadars the case is rare one and not any substantial impact on income could be seen from this case but the cases are not uncommon when we consider it taking an wider population. These small cases will take a shape of uncontrollable mass if the proper authority takes no step to mitigate the problem.

Case No. 9: No share of Produce to Landowner

This is the strongest case among all cases of transgression in barga system. A huge number of Bargadars are not giving legitimate share to their landowners. Majority of this section of Bargadars are not giving share of produce to landowners for several reasons like poor economic condition, bitter relationship with the landowners and political interferences. This type of anomaly can be observed among almost all the categories of Bargadars of all the districts.

In some cases it has been observed that without giving any intimation to the Bargadar, landowner sold out the land to the third party. The Bargadar became angry and denied to give any share of the produce to his new landowner. This type of anomaly has been observed between Medium Scheduled Tribe and Muslim Bargadars of Burdwan district and Semi Medium Scheduled Caste Bargadars of Birbhum District.

On the contrary, as the Bargadar has recorded the land without intimating it to the landowner, the landowner refused to take the share of produce from the Bargadar and protested the manner of recording before the Panchayat. The Panchayat tried to solve this litigation. But the landowner did not agree to accept any mutual arrangements. At last the Panchayat advised the Bargadar to deposit the share of produce in Panchayat office. But mostly due to poor economic condition and political interference, the majority of the Bargadars are not paying due share to the landowners.

The bargadar should be convicted and evicted under Section 17 (C) and Section 16 (2) as discussed in earlier cases.

Table 59A: Distribution of Bargadars under Case No. (9) in Birbhum

Operational Land Holding Category (in Acre)	*Ethnic Groups*				*Total*	*Total Land (in Acre)*
	GC	*SC*	*ST*	*M*		
Marginal	1	8	–	10	19	17.93
Small	–	3	1	1	5	6.60
Semi-medium	–	1	–	–	1	2.95
Medium				1	1	3.24
Large						
Total	1	12	1	12	26	30.72

In Birbhum district, a total of 26 transgressor Bargadars have been found under this anomaly who are holding 30.72 acres of land. Majority of them (73.08%) belong to Marginal farming categories and they are holding the maximum amount of land (58.37%) (Table 59A). In Burdwan district, all total 17 bargadars have been noticed under this case who are holding 24.28 acres of land out of which 15.10 acres are owned land and 9.18 acres are barga land. Majority of them (41.18%) belong to Marginal farmer category but the maximum lands (37.81%) are in the hands of Medium farmer category (Table 59B).

Table 59B: Distribution of Bargadars under Case No. (9) in Burdwan

Operational Land Holding Category (in Acre)	*Ethnic Group*				*Total*	*Barga Land*	*Owned Land*	*Total Land*
	GC	*SC*	*ST*	*M*				
Marginal	–	3	3	1	7	1.89	2.24	4.13
Small	–		2	3	5	2.45	4.00	6.45
Semi–medium	–	–	2		2	1.66	2.86	4.52
Medium	·		1	2	3	3.18	6.00	9.18
Total		3	8	6	17	9.18	15.10	24.28

Table 59C: Distribution of Bargadars under Case No. (9) in Jalpaiguri

Operational Land Holding Category (in Acre)	*GC*	*SC*	*ST*	*M*	*Total*	*Total Land (in Acre)*
Marginal	2	2	14	1	19	8.98
Small	–	–	1	–	1	1.23
Semi-medium	–	2	2	–	4	10.36
Medium	–	–	–	–	–	–
Large	–	–	–	–	–	–
Total	2	4	17	1	24	20.52

In Jalpaiguri 24 Bargadars have been traced out under this case, who are holding altogether 20.52 acres of land. Majority of them belong to Marginal category but maximum land is in the hands of Semi-medium farmers (Table 59C).

Table 60: Demographic Features of the Sample Bargadars under Case No. (9)

(*Average per Household*)

District	*Land Category*	*Family Member*	*Literacy Status (except 0-6 years)*	
			Literate	*Illiterate*
Burbhum	Marginal	6.5	–	5.26
	Small	5	–	4
	Semi-medium	5	–	3
	Medium	6	1	4
Burdwan	Marginal	5.6	2.2	2.4
	Small	6	3	2.12
	Semi-medium	5.5	2.5	2.5
	Medium	4.67	2.67	1.33
Jalpaiguri	Marginal	4.26	0.21	2.89
	Small	4	–	4
	Semi-medium	3.75	0.25	3

The average family size of the bargadar households of Birbhum district is very high. But in case of literacy, all districts are in close proximity (Table 60).

Table 61: Occupation Status of Sample Bargadars under Case No. (9)

District	*Land Category*	*Economic Status*		*Primary Occupation*			*Subsidiary Occupation*	
		Earner	*Dependent*	*Cultivation*	*Business*	*Agri/Daily Labour*	*Agri/Daily Labour*	*Business*
Birbhum	Marginal	2.25	4.25	1	0.25	1	1	–
	Small	2.20	2.80	1	0.20	1	1	0.4
	Semi-medium	1	4	1	–	–	1	–
	Medium	2	4	1	1	–	–	1
Burdwan	Marginal	1.80	3.80	1	0.20	0.6	0.4	0.2
	Small	2.02	3.98	1	0.72	0.3	0.57	0.28
	Semi-medium	1.50	4	1	0.5	–	–	0.5
	Medium	1.33	3.34	1	0.33	–	–	0.67
Jalpaiguri	Marginal	1.63	2.63	1	–	0.63	1	–
	Small	1	3	1	–	–	1	–
	Semi-medium	1.25	2.50	1	0.25	–	0.25	0.25

It is seen from Table 61 that in all three districts, the dependency ratio of Bargadars is very high. Their main source of subsistence remains cultivation. Very few of their family members are engaged in other occupations (Table 61).

Table 62: Land Situation of the Sample Bargadars under Case No. (9)

(Average per Household in Acre)

District	*Land Category*	*Land*		
		Owned	*Leased in*	*Total*
Birbhum	Marginal	–	0.94	0.94
	Small	–	1.32	1.32
	Semi-medium	–	2.95	2.95
	Medium	–	3.24	3.24
Burdwan	Marginal	0.32	0.27	0.59
	Small	0.80	0.49	1.29
	Semi-medium	1.43	0.83	2.26
	Medium	2.00	1.06	3.06
Jalpaiguri	Marginal	–	0.47	0.47
	Small	–	1.23	1.23
	Semi-medium	–	2.59	2.59

In Birbhum district no bargadars have their owned land they only have barga lands, whereas in Burdwan district majority of the Bargdars have their owned land with their Barga land. Again, in Jalpaiguri, all farmers have only barga lands; they don't have any owned lands.

Table 63: Agricultural Support System of the Sample Bargadars under Case No. (9)

District	*Land Category*	*Percentage of Households having*					
		Bullock Cart	*Plough & Bullock*	*Sprayer*	*Thresher*	*Shallow Tube well/ Submersible*	*Tractor/ Power Tiller*
Birbhum	Marginal	–	–	–	–	–	–
	Small	–	–	–	–	–	–
	Semi-medium	–	100.00	–	–	–	–
	Medium	100.00	100.00	–	–	–	–
Burdwan	Marginal	–	–	–	–	–	–
	Small	–	20.00	20.00	–	–	–
	Semi-medium	50.00	100.00	50.00	50.00	–	–
	Medium	33.00	100.00	66.00	33.00	33.00	–
Jalpaiguri	Marginal	–	–	–	–	–	–
	Small	–	–	–	–	–	–
	Semi-medium	50.00	50.00	–	–	–	–

In all three districts, no farmer possesses improved machineries for modern agriculture. Most of the instruments they have are traditional like ploughs and bullocks (Table 63).

In all three districts the economic condition of the Marginal farmers are very painful. Their negative surplus indicates that they have nothing in hands for their reinvestment on agriculture; even they can hardly meet up their family expenses. Probably, besides intention, they are becoming helpless and unable to give share of produce to their landlords (Table 64).

But in case of Semi-medium Bargdars of Birbhum and Jalpaiguri and Semi-medium and Medium Bargadars of Burdwan are not giving the share of produce to their landlords intentionally due their bitter relationship with the landlords.

Table 64: Economic Status of the Sample Bargadars under Case No. (9)

(Average per Household in Rs.)

District	Land Category	In the Past (Annual)				
		From Agriculture		Total Expenditure Status		
		Income	Expenditure	Income	Expenditure	Surplus
Birbhum	Marginal	8260.00	2156.30	12390.00	12437.50	-47.50
	Small	11438.70	3068.16	15119.70	14892.15	227.55
	Semi-medium	27730.50	7227.50	30248.50	25165.90	5082.6
	Medium	30780.00	8352.70	33150.00	30612.45	2537.55
Burdwan	Marginal	8729.35	3509.80	13218.70	13498.35	-279.65
	Small	23145.90	10338.10	26827.90	26711.80	116.10
	Semi-medium	53538.48	22962.30	56588.48	45061.30	11527.18
	Medium	72772.33	30628.45	84317.90	60942.33	23375.57
Jalpaiguri	Marginal	2803.35	983.27	7196.18	7509.31	-313.13
	Small	7782.20	2761.60	9580.20	9437.60	142.60
	Semi-medium	15130.50	5597.00	20191.50	18962.00	1229.50

Case No. 10: Poor Production (but still not evicted)

In general, it has been seen that the productivity of the transgressors are very poor due to several reasons. Most of them belong to the poorest of the poor classes. When they were simply *Bhagchasis* or *Kishans* (sharecroppers) in the field of landowners, they had a good relation with the landowners. At the time of crisis, these landowners acted as "buffer" for them. They could easily take loans at the time of emergencies like crop failure, sowing time, harvesting time, even at the time of non-productive purposes like marriage, illness, drought and flood. Not only that the landowners share major paid-out costs like cost of fertilizers, pesticides, irrigation water etc. at the time of cultivation. But due to recording of land (mostly under the pressure of political parties) this relationship between the sharecroppers and the landowners deteriorated severely. They look each other as their opponents. In these circumstances, the basically poor Bargadars have no option to take easy agricultural loans neither from their landowners nor from other institutional sources like cooperatives or banks due to certain complicacies. After Barga, the government also not supported the

Bargadars with full extent by providing materials or loans even by arranging from other financial institutions. The loans from IRDP had been taken by the Bargadars but most of the money utilized for non-productive purposes. The loans were never repayed. Thus, the Bargadars became defaulters in the eyes of financial institutions. Taking the opportunity, the middlemen and moneylenders extended their hands in support of the poor Bargadars and for that they charge exhorbitant rates in cash or in kinds. All these constraints made the poor Bargadars abstained from giving proper or no share to the landowners. Obviously for this unscrupulous deeds, they had to take shelter of political parties. Their production remains poorer even than the General Bargadars of the locality. According to the rule of Termination of Bargadar (under Section 17 (1), clause (C)), some of the landowners have complained about the situation (low production and under share) to the local panchayat but the panchayat members are totally avoiding this matter. The landowners are keeping silence to avoid political and social litigations with the Party and the Bargadars.

Most of the Marginal and Small and few Semi-medium farmers belong to such anomaly groups.

Total 51 bargadars have been observed in Birbhum under this case, who are holding 63.84 acres of barga lands. They have no owned land on their accounts. Majority (74.51%) of them are Marginal farmers and they are holding the maximum land (56.58%) (Table 65A).

Table 65A: Distribution of Bargdars under Case No. (10) in Birbhum

Operational Land Holding Category (in Acre)	*GC*	*SC*	*ST*	*M*	*Total*	*Total Land (in Acre)*
Marginal	12	8		18	38	36.12
Small	2	3		4	9	16.24
Semi-medium		3		1	4	11.48
Medium				–		
Large				–		
Total	14	14		23	51	63.84

In Burdwan 32 Bargadars have been found under this case who are holding 45.14 acres of land, out of which 17.23 acres are owned land and 27.91 acres are barga land. Among them majority (56.25%) are the Marginal farmers (Table 65B).

Table 65B: Distribution of Bargadars under Case No. (10) in Burdwan

Operational Land Holding Category (in Acre)	*GC*	*SC*	*ST*	*M*	*Total*	*Total Land*	*Owned Land*	*Leased in Land*
Marginal	2	2	1	13	18	10.98	3.78	7.20
Small	1	–	–	5	6	7.62	2.04	5.58
Semi-medium	–	2	–	-	2	4.76	2.14	2.62
Medium	–	5	–	–	5	17.25	8.15	9.10
Large	–	–	–	1	1	4.53	1.12	3.41
Total	3	9	1	19	32	45.14	17.23	27.91

Altogether 49 Bargadars have been observed in Jalpaiguri district under this case, who are holding total 46.84 acres of Barga lands. They have no owned land and majority of them are Marginal farmers (Table 65C).

Table 65C: Distribution of Bargadars under Case No. (10) in Jalpaiguri

Operational Land Holding Category (in Acre)	*GC*	*SC*	*ST*	*M*	*Total*	*Total Land (in Acre)*
Marginal	3	2	23	1	29	8.99
Small	–	3	6	–	9	9.66
Semi-medium	2	2	5	1	10	25.02
Medium	1	–	–	–	1	3.17
Large	–	–	–	–	–	–
Total	6	7	34	2	49	46.84

In most of the cases and in all three districts, the dependency ration is very high and the literacy rate is very low (Table 66).

It is clear from Table 67 that most of the Bargadars are subsistence in nature and their primary occupation is cultivation. Very few of their family members are engaged in other occupations.

The Birbhum and Jalpaiguri Bargadars have no owned land whereas the Burdwan Bargadars have some owned land on their accounts with barga land (Table 68).

Table 66: Demographic Features of the Sample Bargadars under Case No. (10)

(Average per Household)

District	*Land Category*	*Family Member*	*Literacy Status (except 0-6 years)*	
			Literate	*Illiterate*
Burbhum	Marginal	8.82	1.05	7.09
	Small	7.11	1.33	5.34
	Semi-medium	7.00	1.25	5.50
Burdwan	Marginal	6.56	2.17	4.06
	Small	7.33	1.50	5.83
	Semi-medium	6.00	1.50	4.50
	Medium	5.60	1.20	4.40
	Large	11.00	4.00	7.00
Jalpaiguri	Marginal	4.93	0.14	4.07
	Small	5.11	0.33	4.11
	Semi-medium	4.4	1.30	2.30
	Medium	8.00	3	4

Table 67: Occupation Status of the Sample Bargadars under Case No. (10)

District	*Land Category*	*Economic Status*		*Primary Occupation*				*Subsidiary Occupation*	
		Earner	*Dependent*	*Cultivation*	*Service*	*Business*	*Agri/Daily Labour*	*Agri/Daily Labour*	*Business*
Birbhum	Marginal	1.82	7	1	0.03	0.11	0.68	0.95	0.05
	Small	2.00	5.11	1	–	0.33	0.67	1	–
	Semi-medium	1.75	5.25	1	–	–	0.75	1	–
Burdwan	Marginal	1.39	5.17	1	–	–	0.39	0.89	0.11
	Small	1.67	5.66	1	–	–	0.67	0.50	0.17
	Semi-medium	1.50	4.50	1	–	–	0.50	1	–
	Medium	1.20	4.40	1	–	–	0.20	0.80	–
	Large	2	9	1	–	1	–	–	1
Jalpaiguri	Marginal	1.55	3.38	1	–	–	0.55	1	–
	Small	1.89	3.22	1	–	0.22	0.67	0.66	0.33
	Semi-medium	1.60	2.80	1	0.10	0.30	0.20	0.50	0.20
	Medium	1	7	1	–	–	–	–	1

Table 68: Land Situation of the Sample Bargadars under Case No. (10)

(Average per Household in Acre)

District	*Land Category*	*Land*		
		Owned	*Leased in*	*Total*
Birbhum	Marginal	–	0.95	0.95
	Small	–	1.80	1.80
	Semi-medium	–	2.87	2.87
Burdwan	Marginal	0.21	0.40	0.61
	Small	0.34	0.93	1.27
	Semi-medium	1.07	1.31	2.38
	Medium	1.63	1.82	3.45
	Large	1.12	3.41	4.53
Jalpaiguri	Marginal	–	0.31	0.31
	Small	–	1.07	1.07
	Semi-medium	–	2.50	2.50
	Medium	–	3.17	3.17

Table 69: Economic Status of the Sample Bargadars under Case No. (10)

District	*Land Category*	*From Agriculture (Annual)*		*Total Income–Expenditure status (Annual)*		
		Income	*Expenditure*	*Income*	*Expenditure*	*Surplus*
Birbhum	Marginal	8045.74	1588.40	14671.03	14709.70	-38.67
	Small	15462.14	3240.23	17918.50	17621.35	297.15
	Semi-medium	24614.04	5352.78	26845.04	25196.10	1648.94
Burdwan	Marginal	5534.90	1491.50	10195.38	10348.16	-152.78
	Small	11549.89	3125.13	14622.75	14701.20	-78.45
	Semi-medium	21903.62	6203.83	23953.62	22811.55	1142.07
	Medium	31237.68	8926.50	32915.30	31078.12	1837.18
	Large	41494.80	12342.44	44862.00	43435.65	1426.35
Jalpaiguri	Marginal	1856.19	651.73	6948.25	7211.37	-263.12
	Small	6729.85	2319.67	12690.75	12656.00	34.75
	Semi-medium	14370.00	5312.50	20008.00	18939.50	1068.50
	Medium	18106.00	6593.00	26983.00	22109.70	4873.30

In all three districts, the Bargadars' surplus over expenditure (either negative or marginally positive) clearly explains (Table 69) their inability to invest on agriculture properly. In all marginal cases, it is clear that their surplus over expenditure remain negative. They are the worst sufferer of the system. In other cases also, the meager surplus cannot be sufficient to run the agriculture operations smoothly. Therefore, they are under the trap of vicious cycle as mentioned below:

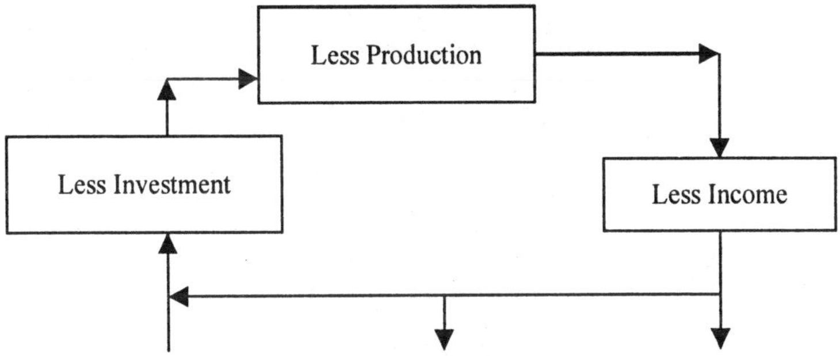

The fundamental phenomenon of Operation Barga (land to the tillers) for better and intensive cultivation and production is thus violated under this case.

Case No. 11: Encroachment of Barga Land by Industries

Encroachment of Barga lands for establishing industries like Tea Industries, Brick industry, Stone Crushing industry etc. are very common in Jalpaiguri. For acquisition of lands, the industrialists used to offer lump sum amount of money or guaranteed job to one family member of the Bargadars.

Table 70: Distribution of Bargdars under Case No. (11) in Jalpaiguri

Operational Land Holding Category (in Acre)	*GC*	*SC*	*ST*	*M*	*Total*	*Total Land (in Acre)*
Marginal	–	–	–	–	–	–
Small	–	–	–	–	–	–
Semi-Medium	–	–	3	–	3	7.11
Medium	–	1	1	–	2	7.24
Large	–	–	–	–	–	–
Total	–	1	4	–	5	14.35

Mostly the Semi-medium and Medium farmers are the victims of such anomalies. In Jalpaiguri this type of anomaly has been observed among 5 bargadars who are holding 14.35 acres of land (Table 70).

Table 71: Demographic Features of the Sample Bargadars under Case No. (11)

(Average per Household)

District	*Land Category*	*Family Member*	*Literacy Status*	
			Literate	*Illiterate*
Jalpaiguri	Semi-medium	5.33	1.33	3.33
	Medium	3.5	1	2.5

Though family size of the anomaly Bargadars are within the limit, the literacy rate is extremely poor (Table 71).

Table 72: Occupation Status of Sample Bargadars under Case No. (11)

(Average per Household)

District	*Land Category*	*Economic Status*		*Primary Occupation*				*Subsidiary Occupation*	
		Earner	*Dependent*	*Cultivation*	*Service*	*Business*	*Agri/ Daily Labour*	*Agri/ Daily Labour*	*Business*
Jalpaiguri	Semi-medium	1.67	3.66	1	0.33	–	0.34	1	–
	Medium	1.50	2	1	–	0.50	–	0.50	0.50

The dependency ratio is moderate and all have primary occupations cultivation. Diversification of occupation has also noticeable due to encroachment of land. The "service" occupation is that service which has been given by the industry (Table 72).

Table 73: Land Situation of the Sample Bargadars under Case No. (11)

(Average per Household)

District	*Land Category*	*In the Past*			*At Present*		
		Owned	*Leased in*	*Total*	*Owned*	*Leased in*	*Total*
Jalpaiguri	Semi-medium	–	2.37	2.37	–	1.26	1.26
	Medium	–	3.62	3.62	–	1.69	1.69

The Bargadars had no owned land previously but they lost a substantial portion of land after encroachment (Table 73) and became uneconomic landholders.

Table 74: Economic Status of the Sample Bargadars under Case No. (11)

(Average per Household)

District	*Land Category*	*In the Past*					*At Present*				
		From Agri		*Total I-E surplus*			*From Agri*		*Total I-E surplus*		
		I	*E*	*I*	*E*	*Surplus*	*I*	*E*	*I*	*E*	*Surplus*
Jalpaiguri	Semi-medium	14360.30	5001.00	16197.00	15013.50	1183.50	7817.20	2397.60	14590.65	14846.00	-255.35
	Medium	22938.40	7361.20	25089.00	18122.50	966.50	9716.75	3513.30	16048.50	15841.75	206.75

After encroachment of barga land in the surplus over expenditures has deteriorated drastically. The negative surplus of semi-medium Bargadar indicates that after few years he will not be in a position to operate his cultivation and will come under the shade of another anomaly like selling out or margining the barga land (Table 74).

Case No. 12: Barga Recording by the Relatives

Only in Jalpaiguri this type of transgression has been found. In these cases it has been noticed that the recording of barga land had been done in the names of some relatives of the landowners, which is extremely illegal.

Table 75: Distribution of Bargadars under Case No. (12) in Jalpaiguri

Operational Land Holding Category (in Acre)	*GC*	*SC*	*ST*	*M*	*Total*	*Total Land (in Acre)*
Marginal	–	–	1	3	4	1.64
Small	–	2	–	–	2	2.38
Semi-medium	1	–	–	–	1	2.57
Medium	–	–	–	–	–	–
Large	–	–	–	2	2	10.22
Total	1	2	1	5	9	16.81

Under this anomaly a total of 9 Bargadars have been found in Jalpaiguri who are holding 16.81 acres of land. Among them majority (above 50%) are Muslims and the majority of the lands are in the hands of large Muslim Bargadars (Table 75).

Table 76: Demographic Features of the Sample Bargadars under Case No. (12)

(Average per Household)

District	*Land Category*	*Family Member*	*Literacy Status (except 0-6)*	
			Literate	*Illiterate*
Jalpaiguri	Marginal	5.5	1.25	3.5
	Small	4	2	2
	Semi-medium	5	2	2
	Large	3.5	3.5	–

Except family size and the literacy rate is somewhat good among these farmers (Table 76).

Table 77: Occupation Status of the Sample Bargadars under Case No. (12)

District	*Land Category*	*Economic Status*		*Primary Occupation*				*Subsidiary Occupation*	
		Earner	*Depen-dent*	*Culti-vation*	*Service*	*Busi-ness*	*Agri/Daily Labour*	*Agri/Daily Labour*	*Busi-ness*
Jalpaiguri	Marginal	2	3.5	1	–	0.5	0.5	1	–
	Small	1.5	2.5	1	0.5	–	–	–	1
	Semi-medium	2	3	1	1	–	–	–	1
	Large	1	2.5	1	–	–	–	–	1

The dependency ratio of all categories of Bargadars are high and very few of other family members are engaged in other occupations. Their main subsistence depends on agriculture (Table 77).

Table 78: Land Situation of the Sample Bargadars under Case No. (12)

District	*Land Category*	*Land (in acres)*		
		Owned	*Leased in*	*Total*
Jalpaiguri	Marginal	–	0.41	0.41
	Small	–	1.19	1.19
	Semi-medium	–	2.57	2.57
	Large	–	5.11	5.11

The Bargadars have no owned land on their account and their subsistence totally depend on their Barga lands (Table 78).

Table 79: Economic Status of the Sample Households under Case No. (12)

District	*Land Category*	*From Agri.*		*Total I-E status*		
		I	*E*	*I*	*E*	*Surplus*
Jalpaiguri	Marginal	2681.20	1161.90	10193.00	9936.75	256.25
	Small	7638.75	3410.35	21846.50	18005.00	3841.50
	Semi-medium	17165.70	7386.00	38916.00	29607.00	9309.00
	Large	33410.25	14078.80	48341.75	33947.50	14394.25

Though surplus over expenditure of marginal bargadars are marginally positive, the same of the other categories is quite better than other categories of transgressions (Table 79).

Case No. 13: Excessive Holding of Barga lands

In these cases the Bargadars are holding barga lands more than the actual stipulated ceiling of holding. It has been found in Jalpaiguri district only.

Sub-section (4) fixes the maximum quantity of land, which a Bargadar shall be entitled to cultivate. Prior to the amendment of sub-section (4) by the West Bengal Land Reforms (Amendment) Act of 1981 the total quantity of land, which a Bargadar could cultivate, was 6.00 hectares (15 acres). Now such quantity has been reduced to 4.00 hectares (10 acres). In computing such area the land owned by the Bargadar as well as the land cultivated by him as Bargadar shall be taken into account.

Sub-section (5) and (6) lay down the consequences of a Bargadar cultivating land in excess of the maximum limit of 4 hectares. When a Bargadar cultivates land in excess of 4 hectares the share of the produce due to him as a Bargadar in respect of the land in excess of 4 hectares shall be forfeited by the State Government by the order made in this behalf by a Revenue Officer.

In the following case the identified Large Bargadars (one belongs to the General Caste and another two belong to Scheduled Castes) are operating a huge amount of land more than 4 hectares (10 acres) (Table 80).

Table 80: Distribution of Bargadars under Anomaly (13) in Jalpaiguri

Operational Land Holding Category (in Acre)	*GC*	*SC*	*ST*	*M*	*Total*	*Total Land (in Acre)*
Large	1	–	2	–	3	38.36
Total	1	–	2	–	3	38.36

Table 81: Demographic Features of the Sample Bargadars under Case No. (13)

District	*Land Category*	*Family Member*	*Literacy Status (except 0-6)*	
			Literate	*Illiterate*
Jalpaiguri	Large	5.00	2.33	2.00

The family size and literacy rate of the Bargadars are fair enough unlike other anomaly Bargadars (Table 81).

Table 82: Occupational Status of the Sample Bargadars under Case No. (13)

District	*Land Category*	*Economic Status*		*Primary Occupation*		*Subsidiary Occupation*
		Earner	*Dependent*	*Cultivation*	*Business*	*Business*
Jalpaiguri	Large	1.67	3.33	1	0.67	0.33

Among these families dependency ratio is high. Diversification of occupation is largely absent. Only one Bargadar is subsidiary engaged in business (Table 82).

Table 83: Economic Status of the Sample Bargadars under Case No. (13)

District	*Land Category*	*From Agri.*		*Total I-E status*		
		I	*E*	*I*	*E*	*Surplus*
Jalpaiguri	Large	83762.90	36413.87	132809.90	78911.30	53898.60

Their high surplus over expenditure of Bargadars clearly gives the indication of their high economic status (Table 83) and that is quite natural because of large operational holding. They are till date not penalized due to the blessings of local politics for holding excessive amount of land over and above ceiling land.

From the entire transgression picture, it could be appeared that the trifle incidences of barga anomalies are rather insignificant if we count the robust canvas of Operation Barga in West Bengal in specific and land reforms in India in general. But all these despicable violations will be magnanimous in near future if the policy makers would not give serious attention to the facts still occurring in the village surroundings. After all, the positive effect of land reforms should go to the people who are tilling the land and toiling to accrue a minimum livelihood out of their primary occupation in the millions of villages.

7

Views of Stakeholders on Barga Anomalies

The following qualitative questions have been asked to the different Stakeholders of the system including the General Bargadars, Non-Bargadars and Bargadars having some kind of anomalies happened with their barga lands. The stakeholders are categorized into seven groups. Different set of questions (related to Barga and the Bargadars' economy) has been asked to each and every category and the responses have been judged in terms of percentages. How many of them (in per cent) are agreed to a particular answer has been given in the parentheses.

The Opinion Groups and the Questions and Respective Responses are as follows:

Group A: Local Government Leaders, Officials and Political Leaders

(Panchayat Pradhan, Panchayat Job assistant, Panchayat Members and Secretary of Local Committee and Panchayat Guard.)

1. **Question**: *What are the causes of indebtedness of the Bargadars ?*

Reponses

(a) Insufficient family income (100%).

(b) After taking loans they have no willingness to repay it. For this they remain indebted through out their life (20%).

(c) After taking emergency loan, and by not repaying the same, the Bargadar becomes a defaulter. To procure further loan he has to dispose of his barga land or to mortgage the land to the moneylender (80%).

2. **Question:** *What is the future of Barga system of cultivation in the State?*

Responses

(a) The barga system has been more or less successful in these areas. Few malpractices could be noticed in recent times due to economic backwardness and poor operational holding of some Bargadars and also some are disposing of the land to avoid the litigation with landowners (55%).
(b) The Bargadars are becoming reluctant to cultivate barga land, as they do not want to share their fruits of labour with the landowners. For this if Government does not take any real step to stop this trend, then the barga system would produce no fruitful result (20%).
(c) After barga recording, the relationship between the Bargadars and the landowners has been deteriorated. This deteriorating relationship have given birth to many anomalies (70%).

3. **Question:** *What kind of impact the barga system producing on village culture* ?

Responses

(a) The lower class people have become more conscious about their rights (30%).
(b) Village integrity has been deteriorated (70%).
(c) Polarization and dividing group-politics has been increased (20%).

4. **Question:** *Why overall production is decreasing under barga system*?

Responses

(a) Most of the Bargadars have their sufficient amount of

owned land. At first they cultivate their owned land and then the barga land. As in case of barga land they have to pay the share of the produce to the landowners, they are not cultivating it with full dedication. Some of them even do not use the landowner's full share of inputs to the barga land. They have a habit of diverting the inputs supposed to be directed to the barga lands in favour of their owned lands (100%).

(b) The Bargadar who have very small operational holding could not able to use inputs in time due to engagement in other occupations (30%).

(c) They are reluctant to share the extent of knowledge about modern agriculture with the landowners (10%).

5. **Question**: *Whether any political help rendered during barga recording?*

Responses

(a) Full political help has been rendered to the Bargadars at the time of barga recording. From procurement of recording documents to its submission, full help has been rendered to the Bargadars (100%).

(b) Many malpractices are being followed while barga recording carried out by the ruling party. For example:
   (i) The political party created undue pressure to the landowners to cultivate the land under barga rules (30%).
   (ii) With the help of political party some landowners have recorded their lands in the name of their labours without intimating them. Till now these Bargadars don't know that they are Bargadars. The landowners are cultivating their lands under their own supervision and management (10%).

6. **Question**: *How many types of violations of Barga rules you have observed among the Bargadars and why they violating the norms?*

Responses

(a) Due to their poor economic condition, some Bargadars

have leased-out their lands to the third party for cultivation (70%).

(b) In exchange of good amount of money or certain percentage of lands the Bargadars have given up the lands to the landowners (20%).

(c) Sometimes the Bargadar takes loan from his landowner keeping the land (with parcha) as mortgage (40%).

(d) With the help of political party some landowners have recorded their land in the name of his labours. The landowners cultivating the lands, which are supposed to be cultivated by the Bargadars (10%).

(e) Some Bargadars do not cultivate the barga land properly. So production of these lands are lower than their owned lands cultivated by the same Bargadars (90%).

(f) Some Bargadars do not give any share of produce to the landowners (70%).

7. **Question**: *What would be the possible remedies to this adverse situation ?*

Responses

(a) Adequate amount of institutional support will have to be provided to the Bargadars (40%).

(b) Measure should be taken to sustain soil fertility (10%).

(c) Small amount of land should be distributed among landless labourers and marginal farmers as barga land (90%).

(d) Literacy status and technological know-how should be increased among the Bargadars (70%).

(e) Political influence on every matter has to be decreased (10%).

(f) Government should take measures through panchayat to increase the production of the barga lands to a certain minimum level and also to ensure the share of the produce in favour of the landlords (40%).

Group – B: Government Officials

(Revenue Inspectors and Office Staff)

1. **Question:** *What are the causes of indebtedness ?*

Responses

(a) Low agricultural production due to small size of operational holding (75%).
(b) Absence of a fixed income source (25%).
(c) Poor knowledge about modern agriculture (75%).
(d) Poverty (75%).
(e) With the introduction of contract system the Bargadar is overburdened with the commitment of the contract and because the production is low he remains in the trap of indebtedness (50%).

2. **Question:** *What is the future of Barga system of cultivation ?*

Responses

Barga system seems to be not fit for the landless agricultural labourers and marginal farmers. But overall the system brought a sense of tenant rights among the cultivators.

3. **Question:** *Whether the R.I. office had to face any political interference during barga recording ?*

Responses

(a) Sometimes the political party members influenced the R.I. officials to record barga land in the name of their own relatives and in the name of their labourers without intimating them, which is illegal (100%).
(b) With the help of political members other than the actual cultivator of lands had recorded their names as Bargadars. Knowing the fact, the R.I. was compelled to do this illegal work (75%).

4. **Question:** *What was the initial procedure of Barga recording ?*

Responses

During the Congress regime barga recording was done on a very low scale. And the share of the produce of landowner and

Bargadar were 66.66 : 33.33 where the landowner provided the inputs and working capital and all labours were supplied by the Bargadars. After 1978 all the permanent labourers were given the status of Bargadars. Prior to 1992 if any cultivator approaches for barga recording the Circle Officer used to record the land (with plot number) in favour of that cultivator, without informing the landowner. During this period the pressure of the political party to the R.I officials was very intense.

5. **Question:** *What remedies would you suggest to improve the situation ?*

Responses

(a) To increase the awareness regarding barga rules and the system of barga of the Bargadars (25%).
(b) Providing consumption loans to the landless and marginal Bargadars during lean season so that they should not be in debt trap or borrow from moneylenders (75%).
(c) Institutional credit should be increased and should be distributed in a proper and improved manner. Non-institutional credit sources should be reduced (100%).
(d) Measures taken to reduce the bitter relationship between the Bargadars and the landowners (50%).

Group – C: Professional Groups

(School Teachers, Doctors and Lawyers)

1. **Question:** *What are the causes of indebtedness of Bargadars?*

Responses

(a) Lack of knowledge of modern cultivation (30%).
(b) Lack of consciousness about financial matters (80%).
(c) Poverty (100%).
(d) Illiteracy (100%).
(e) Lack of sufficient source of income (50%).
(f) Poor investment and income on and from cultivation (16%).

2. **Question:** *What are the sources of the loans for Bargadars?*

Responses

(a) Productive Sources: Arahatdar, Moneylender (local), landowner, fertilizer shops. Purpose-For maintaining agriculture operation.
(b) Unproductive Sources: Moneylender, landowner. Purpose-Festival, Medicine, Marriage, Schooling of children or Emergency purpose.

3. **Question:** *What impact the Barga system has on the village culture ?*

Responses

(a) Integrity and unity among the villagers have been deteriorated (17%).
(b) Political interventions have increased (33%).
(c) Intermingling and cooperation among the villagers has been decreased (50%).

4. **Question:** *Why the production is decreased under Barga system?*

Responses

(a) Lack of knowledge about technological know-how about modern agriculture (70%).
(b) Economic backwardness (50%).
(c) The Bargadars intentionally do not want higher production; if the production would increase then automatically the share of landowners will increase. So they do not want to utilize their full labour capacity. As a result the production of barga land automatically decreased (30%).

Group – D: Bank Officials

1. **Question:** *Why the Bargadars take loans?*

Responses

(a) For cultivation (short term).
(b) For procurement of plough and bullock.
(c) For procurement of cart.
(d) For procurement of thresher, sprayer, pump set.
(e) Loan for rearing of cow, goat and poultry birds.

2. **Question:** *Whether the authenticity of the purpose of loan is maintained ?*

Responses

In case of marginal and small Bargadars, the purpose for which the loan has been taken generally is not maintained. Without creating any asset with the loan it becomes the liability of the Bargadars as well as the bank officials.

3. **Question:** How is recovery rate ?

Responses

At present the provision of short term crop loan is decreased to the Bargadars, because the repayment rate is very poor. Again, in case of short-term loans the Bargadar has an inclination towards non-institutional sources, like local moneylenders, Arhatdar or his own landowner, and this short-term productive loan is taken before the cultivation of the crop.

In case of long-term loan (e.g. procurement of agricultural implements or bullock etc.) there is no fixed time for applying and disbursement. It can be taken at any time within a year when the Bargadar wants the loan.

4. **Question:** *What is the procedure of giving IRDP loans ?*

Responses

Each panchayat has to select 10 cases for loan approval. A joint inspection has been done to each and every beneficiary household constituting a team with the panchayat members, bank official and block representative. Then the list of the beneficiaries is sent to the district level for approval. The approved list then comes from the district level to the block level and to the block level to the panchayat. Another approval is sent from the district level to the bank. Then the duly filled-in form is deposited to the panchayat office by the beneficiaries and the copies of which is sent to the panchayat samity, bank, block, and DRDA. Then the bank disburses the loan after which the beneficiaries can claim for subsidies.

5. **Question**: *With this low recovery situation how the banks trying to recover the defaulted loans* ?

Responses

The bank officials along with the panchayat members/political party members are visiting the houses of the defaulters and are trying to motivate them to repay the loans. Through this process of motivation they are trying to inculcate a consciousness among the beneficiaries and to initiate the sense of responsibility among them. They are trying to convince them that asset creates more assets and liabilities lead to more liabilities. Through this process a positive approach has been initiated among the defaulters (though few in numbers), but in maximum cases it is observed that in the absence of the bank officials, the political party members instigate the defaulters not to repay the loans in order to preserve the vote bank. This is one of the main causes for which IRDP repayment rate is very low.

Group – E: Landowners having Barga lands

1. **Question**: *What are the causes of indebtedness of Bargadars* ?

Responses

(a) Income is not substantial for their sustenance (80%).
(b) Due to bad relationship with the landowners, landowners do not help the Bargadar by providing any assistance to cultivation. So they have to seek loans from non-institutional sources. When they could not repay their loans they are in debt traps (60%).

(c) Due to political backing they are intentionally not repaying the loans they take from institutional sources and remain indebted (40%).

2. Question: *What is the impact of Barga system on village culture?*

Responses

(a) Ego clash between landowner and the Bargadar always exists (100%).
(b) Barga system disintegrated the village society (100%).
(c) Intermingling and co-operation has totally stopped between the landowners and the bargadars (60%).
(d) The barga system of cultivation has demoralized the landowner groups in order to make powerful cultivating labour groups (20%).

3. **Question**: *Why the productions are decreasing under Barga system* ?

Responses

(a) The decision regarding cultivation and its procedure is now totally taken by the Bargadars without consulting the landowners (100%).
(b) During cultivation time the landowner often found the Bargadar is working somewhere else as daily labour. So cultivation could not been carried out at the right time thereby hampering the production level (20%).
(c) Proper supervision of the land before, during and after the cultivation is not done properly by the Bargadars (60%).
(d) Lack of technical know-how among the Bargadars about modern agriculture (80%).
(e) Even if money is given for buying fertilizer and pesticide, proper amount is not been utilized by the Bargadars in the field (80%).
(f) Illiteracy (60%).
(g) Poverty (40%).

4. **Question:** *What remedies do you suggest to improve the situation?*

Responses

(a) Knowledge about modern agricultural operation system should be inculcated among the Bargadars (60%).
(b) Bitter relationship with the landowners should be reduced (100%).
(c) Panchayat should instruct the Bargadars to produce up to a certain level in the barga land otherwise the land might be transferred to the owners (60%).
(d) Cooperation from landowner, especially in regard to production is very much essential (80%).
(e) No marginal or small land should come under barga recording (80%).

Group – F: General Bargadars

1. **Question:** *What are the causes of indebtedness ?*

Responses

(a) Scanty source of income (73.03%).
(b) Lack of co-operation from landowners (40.45%).
(c) Always moneylenders try to entrap Bargadars to encroach the land (12.36%).
(d) Due to emergency loan and inability to repay it (84.27%).

2. **Question:** *Why cultivators gone with the barga system ?*

Responses

(a) Compelled and dragged in by the political party (33.71%).
(b) Cultivating under barga system has been proved to be advantageous to some bargadars as they have procured different loans under various governmental schemes (34.83%).
(c) The landlord has converted the cultivator into Bargadar for his own benefit (12.36%).

(d) Because of security and right to cultivate of land, barga system has been accepted (40.28%).

3. **Question:** *What procedures has been followed in the time of Barga Recording ?*

Responses

(a) Some governmental officers make an inspection of the cultivating land and the bargadars asked about the plot number of his land and the name of the landowner. Then they gave *Kancha Parcha* (Draft Record) to the Bargadar and after this the Bargadar submits this draft record in the Revenue Inspector's (R.I.) office to procure the permanent barga certificate (33.71%).
(b) With the help of the political member the cultivator approaches the settlement officer and fills in the application form for barga recording. After filling the application form the settlement officer gives him an order on that basis the cultivator can go to the settlement office to collect the permanent barga certificate (12.36%).
(c) The panchayat member approaches the cultivator and asks him to fill up the prescribed format for barga recording. After this the cultivator has been asked to come to the panchayat office to collect the permanent barga certificate. He is also told that the landowner will be intimidated there after (34.83%).
(d) First the Bargadar submits the application for barga recording in the R.I. office. Then the application is sent from the R.I. office to the Block Land Reform and Revenue Office (BLR&RO). From the BLR&RO office a date is being fixed for both the cultivator and the landowner for further spot verification and inquiry. After this at a suitable date, the cultivator is asked to collect the permanent barga record certificate from the BLR&RO office (19.10%).

4. **Question:** *Who takes the decision about the selection of crops ?*

Responses

Bargadar himself (100%).

5. **Question**: *With whom the bargadar discusses about cultivation?*

Responses

(a) With no one (39.33%).
(b) With fellow farmers of the village (7.86%).
(c) With fertilizer and pesticide shop (6.74%).
(d) With both (b) and (c) (46.07%).

6. **Question:** *If the landowner wants to sell out the land what would be the bargadar's reaction?*

Responses

(a) "I shall not agree" (34.83).
(b) "If the landowner sells it to me then I will buy it" (40.45%).
(c) "The landowner has to give 1/3rd. of the total land to me" (13.48%).
(d) "Landowner has to pay a lump sum amount to me then I shall allow selling the land"(11.24%).

7. **Question**: *Whether production is decreasing under barga system ? why ?*

Responses

(a) Production is not decreasing (66.29%).
(b) Due to non co-operation of landowners (29.21%).
(c) Due to insufficient supply of family labours (31.46%).
(d) For indebtedness (29.21%).
(e) Lack of agricultural implements (33.71%).

Group – G: Bargadars who have disposed of their lands?

1. **Question:** *What are the causes of indebtedness ?*

Responses

(a) Due to poor operational holding earning from agriculture is too meager to repay the loans (38.71%).

(b) Profit from agriculture has been deteriorating (100%).
(c) No help from landowners (35.48%).
(d) Due to inadequate supply of family labours, we had to engage hired labours. So income from agriculture has again gone down (48.39%).
(e) Moneylender intentionally tried to entrap in debt (80.65%).

2. **Question:** *Source and purpose of the loan.*

Responses

(a) Loans taken for cultivation at the time of crop season.
  (i) Cooperative credit society (9.68%).
  (ii) Arhathdar (64.52%).
  (iii) Fertilizer Shop (45.16%).
  (iv) Moneylender (41.94%).
(b) Loans taken for emergency purposes
  (i) Moneylender (16.13%).
  (ii) Landowner (25.81%).
  (iii) Other village people (67.74%).

3. **Question:** *Whether the production is decreased in Barga system ? why?*

Responses

(a) Due to poor operational holding they have to engage themselves in other occupations for extra earning so they could not give full time for cultivation (38.71%).
(b) Profit from agriculture deteriorated and it is not sufficient to meet up family expenditures (100%).
(c) No help from landowners (35.48%).
(d) Due to insufficient supply of family labours they have to depend on hired labours, which is not possible because of their poor economic condition (48.39%).
(e) Due to inadequate agricultural implements and livestock (74.19%).
(f) As fertilizer cost is increasing so the use of it is decreasing (64.52%).

4. **Question:** *Whether the Bargadars provide share of produce to the landowners?*

Responses

No, the causes are:

(a) Landowner does not take the share (3.23%).
(b) Due to bad relationship with landowner (61.29%).
(c) As landowner stay outside the village, so Bargadar takes the opportunity (16.13%).
(d) Due to poor economic condition (41.44%).
(e) Intentionally (25.80%).

5. **Question:** *If the landowner wants to sell out the land what would be the Bargadar's reaction?*

Responses

(a) Do not agree to sell out the land (68.97%).
(b) Landowner has to give a lump sum amount for disposing of the land (6.90%).
(c) The landowner has to sell the land to the bargadar only (20.69%).
(d) The landowner has to give 1/3rd or half of the land to the bargadar (3.44%).

8

Transgressions with the Patta Holders

The Agri-Patta Holders

According to the Rule 188 of West Bengal Land Reforms Manual, 1991 – Agricultural land [which is at the disposal of Government are settled under the provisions of sub sections (1), (6A) and (5) of section 49 of the W.B.L.R Act, 1955] read with sub-rules (1) to (4) of Rule 20A of the W.B. Land Reforms Rules, 1965) are distributed to persons who want to cultivate such lands personally. Such persons should live within the vicinity of such land. These persons are called Agri-Patta holders.

Table 84: Distribution of Agri-Pattadar in three districts

District	*Total No. of Pattadar*	*Total Patta land holding (in Acre)*	*Average Patta land holding (in Acre)*
Birbhum	284	106.84	0.38
Burdwan	168*	26.77	0.20
Jalpaiguri	860	349.97	0.41

* Including 22 Bargadars who are the holder of 2.09 acres of Patta land also.

In Birbhum total 284 patta holders are holding 106.89 acres of land and their average holding is 0.38 acre. Before taking the possession of patta land all of these persons were landless. Whereas in Burdwan the total patta holding of 168 holders are 26.77 acres and their average holding is 0.20 acre. Among 168 patta holders there are 22 Bargadars also who are holding 2.09 acres of patta land. The rest of the persons were landless before getting the patta land. In Jalpaiguri, 860 Agri-Patta holders have been identified who are holding 349.97 acres of Patta lands with an average of 0.41 acre patta holdings (Table 84).

The Anomaly Cases

In Birbhum out of total patta holders, 59.86 per cent are General Patta Holders who are cultivating their patta land under personal cultivation and have not violated the rules of patta holding ceiling. But 40.14 per cent patta holders are wrapped up with some anomalies like – holding patta land greater than ceiling, leasing out patta lands, selling out patta lands an+d keeping their patta lands fallow.

In Burdwan 64.88 per cent are General Patta holders and 35.12 per cent are anomaly patta holders. Like Birbhum, here all categories of anomalies have been observed except holding patta land greater than ceiling. In Jalpaiguri, 62.33 per cent transgressors have been identified (Table 85).

Table 85: Distribution of General and Anomaly Patta Holders

District	*General Patta Holder*	*Anomaly Patta Holder*	*Total Patta Holder*
Birbhum	170 (59.86)	114 (40.14)	284 (100)
Burdwan	109 (64.88)	59 (35.12)	168 (100)
Jalpaiguri	324 (37.67)	536 (62.33)	860 (100)

Note: Parentheses indicate percentage to total.

Total 4 types of anomalies (deviation from the rules) among the patta holders have been observed in the study area (Table 86).

Case No. 1: Ceiling Surplus Patta Holding

This section of patta holders are holding the patta land more than the ceiling according to 189 (ii) rules of West Bengal Land Reforms Rules – 1965. The rule explains that the maximum area of patta land that may be distributed to a landless person should be one acre. And in case of every patta holder, he only can hold a total of (own and patta or Barga and patta or owned and Barga and patta

Table 86: Distribution of Patta holders according to their Anomalies

District	Patta holding more than ceiling	Total Land (in Acre)	Leasing out Patta land	Total land (in Acre)	Selling out Patta land	Total land (in Acre)	Keeping Fallow Patta land	Total Land (in Acre)	Total No. of Anomaly Patta holder
Birbhum	7 (6.14)	7.285	46 (40.35)	10.38	13 (11.40)	3.09	48 (42.11)	13.44	114 (100)
Burdwan	-	-	37 (62.71)	3.48	18 (30.51)	2.29	4 (6.78)	0.24	59 (100)
Jalpaiguri	1 (0.19)	1.63	150 (27.98)	59.69	279 (52.05)	118.38	106 (19.78)	43.96	536 (100)

Note: Parcenteses indicate percentage to total.

land) one-acre land. This type of anomaly has been observed in Birbhum and Jalpaiguri districts only. In Birbhum, a total of 7 (6.14%) patta holders have been traced out under this anomaly who are holding average 1.04 acres patta land. In Jalpaiguri only one case has been found under this anomaly. These anomalies have occurred due to political compulsion. This section of patta holders are mainly Agriculture/Daily labourers. They have no agricultural support system. They cultivate their lands casually. Their agricultural production is very poor. Their main moto of cultivating this land is, producing paddy for home consumption and not for increasing production or selling some amount of produce. For this their investment on cultivation is also very low. Their main sources of income are still now their Agriculture/Daily labour occupations. They cultivate their lands only in Kharif season.

Case No. 2: Leasing out Patta Land

These section of patta holders are leasing out their patta lands to the landowners of the contiguous lands on contract basis. As they are not cultivating these lands, so they should be convicted under the rule no. 188 (i) of W.B.L.R Rules, 1965, where it has been stated, "Agricultural lands are distributed to persons who want to cultivate such lands personally."

In Birbhum this type of anomaly has been observed among 46 (40.35% out of total) patta holders. Whereas in Burdwan it has been observed among 37 (62.71% out of total) patta holders. In Jalpaiguri, 150 cases (27.98 per cent of total patta holders) are found holding 59.69 acres of lands.

All this section of patta holders are mostly agricultural labourers. They have no agricultural support mostly system and proper knowledge of agricultural operation management. For this they have no intrinsic urge to cultivate these lands. According to Government policy they got the possession of these lands. As they have no investment capacity, knowledge of agricultural operation management and agricultural support system, so their production remain very poor at the initial stage of holding these lands. For this they have leased out it for getting some benefit from this without any investment.

Case No. 3: Selling out Patta Land

Like the Bargadars, this section of patta holders are selling out their lands in exchange of some money to some rich farmers (among them some was the actual landowners of that land before the vesting of his land) with or without some written document internally. This section of patta holders should be convicted under the rule no. 188 (i) of W.B.L.R Rules, 1965.

In Birbhum 13 (11.40% out of total) patta holders have been traced out whereas in Burdwan 18 (30.51% out of total) patta holders have been traced out under this case. In Jalpaiguri 279 cases (52.05 per cent) have been identified who are handling 118.38 acres of patta land and entangled with these cases.

Case No. 4: Keeping Patta Land as Fallow (uncultivated)

This section of patta holders are keeping their patta lands fallow in all seasons. These lands have no utility to them. This section also should be convicted under the rule no. 188 (i) of W.B.L.R Rules, 1965.

In Birbhum, this type of anomaly has been observed in 48 (42..11%) patta holders, whereas in Burdwan it has been observed among 4 (6.78%) patta holders. In Jalpaiguri, 106 cases have been found who are holding 43.96 acres of patta lands. These patta holders have no ability to cultivate their patta lands. They are very poor, illiterate and mainly engaged in agriculture/daily labour activities. At the initial stage they have tried to cultivate these lands but stopped it due to poor return.

9

Summary and Policy Intervention

In West Bengal a series of tenancy reform measures were undertaken since the introduction of Bargadari Act 1950. In the Act the Bargadars (sharecroppers) were recognized as some kind of under tenant. This Act recommended 60 : 40 shares in favour of such bargadars who would be responsible for supplying manual labours, draught power, seeds and manures. However, there was no provision for the protection of Bargadar's occupancy rights at the time of West Bengal Estate Acquisition Act, 1954, was promulgated. The primary motive was that to abolish all intermediary rights on land, which the Zamindars were enjoyed from the period of permanent settlement in 1793. In the West Bengal Land Reform Act in 1956, provisions were made to protect the sharecroppers from gross exploitation on-the part of big landowners. For this reason an amendment of the Bargadari Act was made and share ratio has been changed from 60 : 40 to 75 : 25 in favour of the sharecroppers. These Acts, specially, the Bargadari Act, 1972, were no doubt radical for safeguarding the interest of the Bargadars.

When the Left Front government came to power in West Bengal in 1977, the government immediately tried to implement the land reform measures, specially, the tenancy reform measures i.e. the Bargadari Act of 1972. Envisaging the helplessness of the Bargadars, the government decided to implement the provisions of the Bargadari Act in favour of the sharecroppers through a movement called **Operation Barga**.

The net result, the socio-economic conditions of the allottees have improved, with regard to income, employment, education, housing and social prestige, as direct result of land distribution. However, the fact remains that the landlords had lost some economic assets, may be marginal in comparison to their overall property is concern, but the landless who did not have any productive assets at all, gained substantially.

However, all was not well in the land distribution programmes. The allottees have suffered because of the procedural delays, judicial decisions, lack of inputs, capital and technological know-how and overall indifference towards the comparatively weaker sections. Because of these constraints, some peculiar and interesting dimensions of Operation Barga have been observed in West Bengal. They are given below:

(a) Numerous cases have been found where crop sharing has not implemented as per the law and often it goes against the Bargadars' interests.
(b) Mutual arrangements between landlords and the Bargadars are widespread and for that reason neither peasants' organization nor the Panchayat take appropriate measures for intervene into the cases. There is also random politicking with land reform measures.
(c) It has been observed that sometimes the Bargadar compelled to return the barga land to the landowners. It is also found that, landowners sometimes sell the barga land to a third party by taking informal consent (no-demand) from the bargadar.

The tillers of the land, having usufructuary rights over land often dispose of their recorded lands in favour of the landowners (or to a third party), defeating the very objective of Operation Barga. These reverse processes, along with other reactionary tendencies, are now gaining ground in West Bengal, which remains a model of land reform programme to the country till today.

It has been observed from the qualitative judgements of the study that the middle class and semi-middle/medium class landholders, who were otherwise employed, used to act as the "buffer" between the farmer/Bargadar and the middlemen/*Arhatdar* to avoid distress sell of their produce. This class, for various reasons, withdrew themselves from farm operation, placing the Bargadar at the mercy of the middlemen, which ultimately force them to compromise with their rights and compelled them to take unlawful measures transgressing the rules and regulations of Barga. The common transgressons found in the study area are as follows:

Case 1 : Subleasing of Baga Land to the Third Party
Case 2 : Mortgaging Barga land
Case 3 : Selling out Barga land
Case 4 : Political Eviction
Case 5 : Forceful Acquisition of Barga land by landowner
Case 6 : Cultivating Barga land through Mutual understanding
Case 7 : Mutual Distribution of Barga land between all the heirs after the death of Bargadar
Case 8 : Use of Barga land in Non-agricultural purpose
Case 9 : No share of produce to landowner
Case 10: Poor production of Barga land but not evicted
Case 11: Encroachment of barga land
Case 12: Leasing in Barga land
Case 13: Others

Policy Implications and Interventions

From the entire research work done in three representative districts of West Bengal, it has been found that a number of transgressions (anomalies) in the barga system exist. For that the benefit of the barga system has not been properly distributed to the ultimate users of the system with whom the operation (barga) had been carried out as a political movement by the ruling Left Front Government of West Bengal. The trend of transgressing is increasing and in near future the system will be more corruptive and will become infructuous. Even the taking of further course of action will be difficult such as consolidation of holding and cooperative farming. Though, the emphasis and importance of land reforms in the State is already declining, still it is the only major success of the Left Front government towards the upliftment of rural people in millions of villages in all sense. To continue the operation and distribution of benefits in favour of actual tillers of lands some policies has to be taken up by the government to foolproof the system. In the following areas some interventions are needed in an urgent basis:

1. It has been found from the study that instead of augmenting agricultural productivity, often the system appeared as a barrier to the productive forces and due to

lack of incentive the lands are not been potentially used either by landowners or by the Bargadars.

2. A psychological gap of misunderstanding exists between the landowners and the Bargadars and it is widespread. It ruins the culture of agriculture in the rural areas.
3. The Bargadars are being devoid of non-agricultural income generating activities as because they have recorded their lands, so they are supposed to gain from the agriculture.
4. Previously the middle class landowners were acting as "buffer" for the agricultural tenants. They had a very good relationship with the tenants. At the time of their need the landowners used to help them with all efforts. They used to provide consumption loans, loans for emergency purposes and working capital for cultivation. At the very moment, the tenant went for recording of his barga land the relationship has been broken and the landowner perceived a psychological set back. Very few landowners were so generous to take the issue sportingly.
5. As a result, the Bargadars had to sacrifice the owners' help as well as he has not been provided with assured institutional help from the government. The situation of the Bargadars became simply helpless.
6. The Bargadars have no ideas about the ultimate motto of land reforms and Operation Barga and they are only satisfied with their tenancy rights.
7. Political interference in the entire process is tremendous and in many cases it hampers the productivity by creating willful defaulters of the system.
8. The Act of Land Reform does not provide enough security to the Bargadars and it has been established from the study that in a number of cases the Bargadars were deprived of by the landowners, by the party leaders and by the unscrupulous land agents.
9. The general condition of the Bargadars are miserable and they are not in a position to carry out their businesses with enthusiasm. So barga, in that regard, could not bring much economic change among the Bargadars in the state.

Therefore, it is necessary to review the entire system and objectives in the context of present transformation and global change.

Bibliography

Allen, Franklin (1995): *On the Fixed Nature of Sharecropping Contracts*. The Economic Journal, 95, 30-48.

Bagchi, Amiya Kumar (1976): *Cropsharing Tenancy and Neoclassical Economics*. Economic and Political Weekly, January.

Bandopadhyaya, Nripen (1981): *'Operation Barga 'and Land Reforms Perspective in West Bengal: A Discursive Review*. Economic and Political Weekly, Review of Agriculture, June.

Bandopadhyaya, Nripen and Associates (1983): *Evaluation of Land Reform Measures in West Bengal-A Report* (Monograph). Centre for Studies in Social Sciences, Calcutta.

Banerjee and Ghatak, M. (1995): *Empowerment and Efficiency: The Economics of Tenancy Reforms*. Mimeograph, Department of Economics, Harvard University.

Bardhan, P.K. and Rudra, A. (1985): *The Domain of Rural Labour Markets: Results of a Survey in West Bengal, 1981-82*. Economic and Political Weekly, Vol. 20, December.

Bardhan, Pranab (1970): *Trends in Land Relations: A Note*. Economic and Political Weekly, Annual Number, January.

Bardhan, Pranab (1976): *Variations and Extent and Forms of Agricultural Tenancy-II: Analysis of Indian Data across Regions and Over Time*. Economic and Political Weekly, September.

Bhaduri, A. (1973):*A Study in Agricultural Backwardness Under Semi-feudalism*. The Economic Journal, Vol. 83, No. 329, March.

Bhaduri, A. (1983): *Economic Structure of Backward Agriculture*. Academic Press, London.

Bharadwaj, K. (1985): *A View on Commercialisation in Indian Agriculture and the Development of Capitalism*. Journal of Peasant Studies, Vol. 12, No. 4, July.

Bharadwaj, K. and Das, P.K. (1975): *Tenurial Conditions and Modes of Exploitation: A Study of Some Villages in Orissa*. Economic and Political Weekly, Annual Number, Vol. 10, February.

Bhaumik, Sankar Kumar (1993): *Tenancy Relations and Agrarian Development: A Study of West Bengal*. Sage Publications. New Delhi.

Bose, S.R. (1974): *The Comilla Cooperatives Approach and the Prospects for Broad-based Green Revolution in Bangladesh*. World Development, Vol.2, No.8, August.

Byres, T.J. (ed.) (1983): *Sharecropping and Sharecroppers*. Frank Cass, London.

Chakravarty, Aparajita and Rudra, Ashok (1973): *Economic Effects of Tenancy: Some Negative Results*. Economic and Political Weekly, July.

Chakravorty, S. (1979): *On the Question of Home Market and Prospect of Indian Growth*. Economic and Poltical Weekly, Annual Number.

Chandra, Nirmal K. (1974): *Farm Efficiency under Semi-Feudalism: A Critique of Marginalist Theories and Some Marxist Formulations*. Economic and Political Weekly, Special Number, August.

Chattopadhyay, Manabendu (1979): *Relative Efficiency of Owner and Tenant Cultivation: A Case Study*. Economic and Political Weekly, Review of Agriculture, September.

Chattopadhyay, Suhas (1979): *Operation Barga: A Comment*. Economic and Political Weekly, Review of Agriculture, December.

Cheung, Steven S. (1969): *Theory of Share Tenancy*. University of Chicago Press, Chicago.

Choudhury, P. Roy (1980): *Land Reforms: Promises and Fulfillment*. Economic and Political Weekly, December.

Dasgupta, Biplab (1984): *Sharecropping in West Bengal: From Independence to Operation Barga*. Economic and Political Weekly, Review of Agriculture, June.

Dutt, Kalyan (1981): *Operation Barga: Gains and Constraints*. Economic and Political Weekly, Vol. 16, Nos. 25-26, Review of Agriculture, June.

Dwivedi, Harendranath and Rudra, Ashok (1973): *Economic Effects of Tenancy: Some Further Negative Results*. Economic and Political Weekly, July.

Ghosh, A.K. (1983): (ed.) *Agrarian Reform in Contemporary Developing Countries*. Croom Helm, London.

Ghosh, Ratan (1981): *Agrarian Programme of Left Front Government*. Economic and Political Weekly, Review of Agriculture, June.

Government of West Bengal (1998): *Land Reforms in West Bengal*.

Joshi, P.C. (1987): *Institutional Aspects of Agricultural Development: India from Asian Perspective*. Allied Publishers Private Ltd, Ahmedabad.

Khasnabis, Ratan (1981): *Operation Barga: Limits to Social Democratic Reformism*. Economic and Political Weekly, Vol. 16, Nos. 25-26, Review of Agriculture, June.

Khasnabis, Ratan (1982): *Operation Barga: A Further Note*. Economic and Political Weekly, Vol. 17, Nos. 26, September.

Khasnabis, Ratan (1986): *A Treatise on the Concept of the Semi-Feudalism and India's Agrarian Economy* (in Bengali). People's Publishing Society, Calcutta.

Konar, Hare Krishna (1980): *Agricultural Problem in India* (in Bengali). National Book Agency Private Ltd, Calcutta.

Lahiri, R.K.(1999): *Status of Land Reforms in the Sub-Continent*. (Unpublished paper presented in the Conference on Status of Land Reforms in South Asia), South-South Solidarity, New Delhi.

Laxminarayan, H. and Tyagi, S.S. (1977): *Inter-State Variations in Types of Tenancy*. Economic and Political Weekly, Review of Agriculture, September.

Lehman, D. (1985): *Sharecropping and capitalist Transition: Some Evidence from High Lands of Equdator*. Centre of Latin American Studies, Working Paper.

Lieten, G.K. (1990): *Depeasantisation Discontinued: Land Reforms in West Bengal*. Economic and Political Weekly, October.

Mahalanobis, P.C. (1963): *Social Transformation and the Scientific Base of Economic Growth*. Sankya, B.25 (1) (2).

Marshall, A. (1961): *Principles of Economics*. Macmillan, London.

Marx, Karl (1974): *Capital: A Critique of Political Economy*. Vol. III, Ed: by Frederick Engels, Lawrwnce and Wishhart, London.

Mathur, M.P. (1988): *Land Distribution: Success or Failure* ! Yojana, February 16-29.

Mishra, Tushar Kanti (1988): *Land Reforms in Bihar*. Kuruksehtra, June.

Mukherjee, K.K. *et. al.* (1999): *Status of Land Reforms in South Asia: Focus on India, Bangladesh and Nepal*. (Unpublished Status Paper presented in the Conference on Status of Land Reforms in South Asia), South-South Solidarity, New Delhi.

Murty, C.S. (1998): *Land Lease Market in Agriculture*. Commonwealth Publishers, New Delhi.

Nadkarni, M.V. (1976): *Tenants from the Dominant Class: Developing Contradiction in Land Reforms*. Economic and Political Weekly, Review of Agriculture, December.

Narain, Dharam and Joshi, P.C. (1969): *Magnitude of Agricultural Tenancy*. Economic and Political Weekly, Review of Agriculture, September.

Newbery, D.M.G. (1975): *Tenurial Obstacles to Innovation*. Journal of Development Studies, Vol. II, No. 4.

Pal, Sasanka Sekhar (1992): *Impact of Tenancy Reforms on Production and Income Distribution – A Case Study of Operation Barga in West Bengal* (Unpublished Project Report), Palli Charcha Kendra, Visva-Bharati.

Patnaik, Utsa (1979): *Neo-Populism and Marxism: The Chyanovian View of the Agrarian Questions and its Fundamental Fallacy*. Journal of Peasant Studies, Vol. 6, No. 4, July.

Rahman, H.Z. (1994): *Re-thinking the Land Reform Question*. Proceedings of the Workshop on Bangladesh Agriculture in the 21st Century, Dhaka.

Raju, K.N. (1997): *Land Reforms in India: Achievements and Failures*. Kuruksehtra, August.

Rao, V.M. (1972): *Land Transfers in Rural Communities: Some Findings in a Ryotwari Region*. Economic and Political Weekly, Review of Agriculture, September.

Ray, Debidas (1978): *The Small Lessor and the Big Lessee: Evidence from West Bengal*. Economic and Political Weekly, Review of Agriculture, December.

Reid, J.D. (1976): *Sharecropping and Agricultural Uncertainty*. Economic Development and Cultural Change, Vol. 24, No. 3.

Robertson, A.F. (1987): *The Dynamics of Productive Relationships: African Share Contracts in Comparative Perspective*. University Press, Cambridge.

Rogaly, Ben, Harriss-White, Barbara and Bose, Sugata (Ed.) (1999): *Sonar Bangla: Agricultural Growth and Agrarian Change in West Bengal and Bangladesh*. Sage Publications, New Delhi. Annual Report 2003-04: Ministry of Rural Development, Government of India.

Rudra, Ashok (1981): *One Step Forward, Two Steps Backward.* Economic and Political Weekly, Vol. 16, Nos. 25-26, Review of Agriculture, June.

Saha, Bimal Kumar (1999): *Land Reform and Agrarian Question in Bangladesh.* (Unpublished paper presented in the Conference on Status of Land Reforms in South Asia), South-South Solidarity, New Delhi.

Sanyal, S.K. (1972): *Has There Been a Decline in Agricultural Tenancy?* Economic and Political Weekly, May.

Sen, Bhawani (1962): *Evolution of Agrarian Relations in India.* People's Publishing House, New Delhi.

Sengupta, Sunil (1981): *West Bengal Land Reforms and the Agrarian Scene.* Economic and Political Weekly, Vol. 16, Nos. 25-26, Review of Agriculture, June.

Siddique, K.U. (1979): *A Comment on Jannuzi and Peach: A Note on Land Reform in Bangladesh.* The Journal of Peasant Studies, Vol. 6, No. 3, April.

Smith, Adam (1969): *The Wealth of Nations.* Ed. by Andrew Skinner, Pelican Classics.

Swain, Mamta (1998): *Peasant Agriculture and Share Tenancy in Orissa (Examining Neoclassical and Marxist Approach).* Commonwealth Publishers, New Delhi.

Umar, B. (1982): *On Land Reforms in Bangladesh.* Sanskriti, Vol. 5, October, Dhaka.

Williams, Glyn (1999): Panchayati Raj and the Changing Micro-Politics of West Bengal. In Ben Rogaly, Barbara Harriss-White and Sugata Bose (ed.) (1999): *Sonar Bangla: Agricultural Growth and Agrarian Change in West Bengal and Bangladesh.* Sage Publications, New Delhi.

Winters, D.L. (1978): *Farmers Without Farms: Agricultural Tenancy in Ninteenth Century Iowa.* Greenwood Press, Westport.

Index